Think Indigo

A Blueprint for B2B *Product* Marketing Success

Amy Mikolasy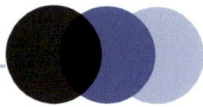

Copyright © 2025 Amy Mikolasy.
All rights reserved.

No part of this book may be used, reproduced, translated, electronically stored, or transmitted in any form, by any means without prior written permission of the publisher, except as provided by United States of America copyright law and fair use.

ISBN: 979-8-3032-0002-9 (print hardcover)

First edition.
Printed in the United States of America.

Cover design by Contrast & Co., Annapolis, Maryland U.S.A.

Contents

Acknowledgements and Dedication
Preface

1	**Empowerment Starts Here**	1
	Architect a Leading Plan That Inspires	
2	**Build a Solid Foundation**	9
	Do Three Things with One Objective	
	Know Your Audience, Value and Voice	
	Understand the Strategic Priorities	
3	**Create a Repeatable Framework**	43
	Align Campaigns and Content	
	Craft a Story That Resonates	
	Integrate Your Marketing Tactics	
	Spotlight the Meaningful Metrics	
4	**Be Passionate About …**	83
	Design	
	Details	
5	**Go-To-Market with Confidence**	93
	Model a Launch Strategy	
	Sell the Sellers	
6	**Look Up**	115
	Help Others Find Their Marketing Voice	
	Learn to Pivot	
	The Right Team, Tools, and Budget	
	UX is Really Just Good Marketing	
	Find Your Sweet Spot	

About the Author   143
Index   145

Acknowledgements and Dedication

Authoring a book is hard. So, thank you AI. Specifically, ChatGPT, the artificial intelligence chatbot developed by OpenAI. I'm extremely grateful for the impressive assistance you delivered in helping me to enrich and edit content. For me personally, you truly made the writing process so much easier, faster, and better.

To all my esteemed colleagues and mentors, past and present, thank you for sharing your passion, knowledge, expertise, and friendship with me. This book is dedicated to you - and to the many years of inspiration, support and collaboration that have shaped my career in business, product, amd marketing.

To Ted, whose talks, creativity, and encouragement inspired me to think outside the box and take on new challenges with confidence.

To my talented guest contributors - Saul, Jessica, Peter, and MJ. Marketing is undeniably a team effort, and your invaluable ideas and influences are immensely respected and appreciated.

To the stunning design work and contribution of Contrast & Co., your artistic vision and ingenuity have been a powerful inspiration. Your ability to craft a visual identity that perfectly captures the story's essence is nothing short of remarkable.

And to you, my audience. I pass along my insight and experience if you can benefit from it too. I hope this book helps you shape and navigate your own marketing world more clearly and easily.

Preface

I once heard someone describe that there are three phases to a career: Learning, Earning and Wisdom. It resonated quite deeply with me. And as I entered the Wisdom phase of my own career, I realized the wealth of insight, experiences, and information I had accumulated, in addition to a fluency in navigating within the profession that I loved. It was hard-earned knowledge that I felt excited about sharing, especially when it might be of benefit to the next wave of Learners and Earners in my field.

Looking back, as the daughter of a lifelong Bell Labs engineer, I was perhaps one of the very first junior high school girls to make a mobile call, well before cellular was widely available. I jokingly take credit for helping to start an amazing trend, but it was the experience that sparked my passion for technology.

Fast forward several decades, and over 25 years immersed in marketing and product within the tech industry, I owe much of my success to mentors – some knowingly, others unwittingly – who generously shared their wisdom with me.

This book is my way of paying it forward, encapsulating and passing along some of the best of my own insights and revelations. The chapters ahead offer personal perspectives. While not everything in this guide may be universally applicable, I offer it humbly in the hope it may be of benefit to you.

If you find yourself navigating the wildly dynamic intersection of marketing, product, and sales in the B2B technology realm, this book is tailored for you. I hope you find value in these pages.

Best regards,

Amy

1

Empowerment Starts Here

In a buyer-led digital world, business-to-business (B2B) marketing is **too complex not to have a plan**. The challenges are tough, and the environment can be chaotic.

It's not a secret that one of the biggest difficulties that marketing teams face today is the nonstop evolving nature of the marketing landscape. In addition, the way that people consume and engage with marketing content is constantly shifting. Our job is not easy, and trying to stay on top of this rapidly changing dynamic presents a multitude of hurdles.

- **Keeping up with the latest trends and technologies**: With fresh marketing channels and technologies emerging all the time, it can be difficult for marketing teams to stay up-to-date and effectively leverage these tools to reach their target audience.
- **Measuring return-on-investment (ROI)**: With so many different channels and touchpoints involved in modern marketing, it can be difficult to measure the impact of marketing efforts and determine the ROI of specific campaigns. Marketing teams must find ways to track and analyze customer behavior across multiple channels, and attribute revenue to specific marketing activities.
- **Rising above the noise**: With so much competition in the marketplace, building brand loyalty and

retaining customers is more important than ever. Marketing teams must find ways to rise above the noise, create emotional connections with their audience and foster long-term relationships that go beyond a single transaction.

- **Managing data and privacy concerns**: With increasing concern over data privacy and security, marketing teams must ensure that they are collecting, storing, and using customer data in a responsible and ethical manner that complies with global laws and regulations. This requires a deep understanding of data privacy regulations and a commitment to transparency and trust-building with customers.

With so much ground to cover, whether you are a marketing executive, manager, or leader, **it's easy to feel, at times, extremely overwhelmed**.

- Marketing teams can become inundated by the **constant pressures of operational work** and demands, often random, reactive, frantic, and fragmented. As a result, they can easily lose track of the bigger picture and struggle to gain control.
- Working in **an environment without a clear structure, at times quite common, can cause a lot of stress** for marketers. There may be multiple teams communicating independent messages about their specific business unit, product, or service. It can lead to confusion and a frustrating inconsistency in the messaging being delivered to the market.
- **Misalignment among sales and marketing teams** is an age-old issue that still leads to tension in many organizations, often stemming from a lack of communication between the two functions. It's no longer viable for these two groups to remain divergent and achieve strong performance. When there is a dislike or a disconnect here, it can lead to

missed opportunities, reduced efficiency, and a negative impact on the customer experience.
- In a digital world where we are constantly bombarded with an overwhelming amount of information from various sources, it can be challenging for marketers too, to filter out what is important and relevant. **Information overload can lead to feelings of overwhelm and anxiety, which can impact our ability to make informed decisions and act.** It can also lead to a decrease in productivity, as individuals may spend more time sifting through information rather than focusing on completing tasks.

Architect a Leading Plan That Inspires

As the marketing world is vast with this constant change, challenges, opinions, and information everywhere, sometimes it's not so easy to figure out where to begin and what to do. It's common to wonder: Where do you start? How do you design a plan? How do you navigate? How do you control the chaos? This book is an opportunity to take a step back and view things from a broader perspective. **A guide to help you frame your approach to marketing more holistically - with sound strategy, practical application, and fresh ideas.**

This is how I have been successful at embracing the chaos. Navigating through noisy, crowded spaces to become visible. It focuses not on revealing new types of marketing tactics, but how to 'curate' and build a versatile and effective plan that encompasses them.

> "Simplicity is the ultimate sophistication."
> - Leonardo da Vinci

With this approach, you can more easily focus on building integrated campaigns centered in the buyer's journey, bringing sales into the conversation and inspiring cross-functional collaboration.

Ultimately, it's all about generating revenue and securing the budget you need. Delivering quality leads, and enough of them. Producing engaging content and ensuring your work is getting the recognition and rewards you would expect it to.

Achieving this demands prioritization, focus, and a well-crafted plan. A robust plan provides a sense of control, not only over your marketing endeavors and their outcomes, regardless of scale, but also over the course of your day. There's a notable saying: if you fail to plan your time, someone else will take charge of it for you. Likewise, if you're not diligently executing your own plan, you may find yourself implementing someone else's.

Now more than ever, a unified marketing and messaging plan is essential for any company looking to build a strong brand and drive long-term success. According to one popular trend report, organized marketers are 397% more likely to report success.[1] That's an impressive number. By aligning teams around a common goal and creating a clear and consistent story, companies can differentiate themselves in a crowded marketplace and build strong relationships with their customers. A unified marketing and messaging strategy can allow teams to work more efficiently and effectively, reducing duplication of effort and ensuring that resources are being used in the most impactful way possible.

Modern digital marketing is not easy. But remember, it's still marketing. You need to:

- Target your market.
- Understand what they care about.

---

[1] 'Trend Report, Marketing Strategy 2022', CoSchedule, accessed February 7, 2024, https://coschedule.com/marketing-statistics.

- Connect to them with your message.
- Improve your image.
- Drive sales.

You may just use a vast number of different (and constantly evolving) tactics, platforms, tools, and methodologies to do it.

The concept of how to "Think Indigo" is simple. Yet when executed, it can be quite powerful. It's about always starting with a plan – an Indigo Blueprint. A creative presentation that provides insight and clarity (Indigo), while organizing and curating your marketing initiatives into a clear program - that can be easily communicated across teams (the Blueprint).

> Don't just do a marketing plan,
> architect an inspiration.

Why Indigo? It's the color of wisdom, insight, and intuition. It gives an ability for planning the future and is often associated with clarity and a clear mind. Indigo is a deep and rich color that is often used to convey a sense of elegance, sophistication, and intelligence. It can also be used to evoke a sense of trust and dependability.

Why a Blueprint? As we know, blueprints are a type of technical drawing or plan that are used in various fields, including architecture, engineering, and construction. They're useful and applicable to marketing for several reasons. Firstly, they provide a clear and accurate **visual representation of what is being built**, which helps ensure that the design and construction are done correctly and to the necessary standards. Secondly, **blueprints facilitate communication** of the ideas and designs effectively to clients, contractors, and other stakeholders. This helps to ensure that everyone involved is on the same page and has a clear understanding of what is being done, and what is needed. And thirdly, blueprints are useful simply for project planning and management, as they provide a detailed and accurate record of the design and process. This is always useful for tracking, identifying potential issues or challenges, and making necessary adjustments as the plan proceeds.

> As you delve into the chapters ahead,
> there are two important things to keep in mind.

During a casual exchange of ideas with a favorite colleague of mine, Saul Einbinder, we found ourselves talking about the importance of setting the right stage upfront. Saul, a seasoned entrepreneurial executive with deep roots in high-tech and marketing, has transitioned into a role where he now shares his vast strategic insights as a technology lecturer. With his characteristic dry wit and sharp intellect, he offered a simple piece of advice: "Tell the story of the shift in B2B marketing, from the old way to the new."

He was right. In my experience, I've witnessed firsthand the evolution from the old way, where B2B marketing teams were often relegated to the role of reactive service providers, scrambling to respond to siloed requests from various business units. This disjointed approach led to a scattershot array of marketing efforts - random acts of marketing with little cohesion or strategic direction.

Saul's insight made me realize the importance of highlighting the stark contrast with today's more evolved approach. The new way is not just a shift; it's a transformation. It's about moving from reactive, disjointed activities to a unified, strategic mindset. Today's successful B2B marketing teams operate with intentionality, coherence, and a clear vision that drives every action.

Yet, the old way still lingers in some corners of the industry, more often than we might like to admit. That's where this book comes in - it's a guide for teams ready to make the leap from yesterday's tactics to tomorrow's triumphs, equipping them with the confidence and control needed to thrive in this new marketing landscape. That said, these are the two essential points to note.

> First, it's crucial to understand that you don't have to do everything – and nor should you.

The information in this book is rich and exciting, but it can also be quite overwhelming.

There are countless marketing channels and strategies, but that doesn't mean you need to master them all. You may wonder if it's necessary to implement every idea that comes your way. The answer is no. You can't - and shouldn't - try to execute every marketing tactic simultaneously.

Accepting this will help you focus on what truly matters, allowing you to go deep rather than wide. Trying to do too much spreads your resources thin and makes it impossible to gain deep insights or achieve long-term results. Additionally, success doesn't require mastering every platform or tool - just the ones that fit your strategy and business.

Remember, your plan doesn't need to be fully realized from the outset. It can start with a focused, manageable scope and gradually expand as you gain insights and resources. By starting small and building momentum, you can scale your efforts strategically, ensuring each phase adds value and supports long-term success.

> Second, it's wise to acknowledge that when it comes to marketing, everyone has an opinion.

The truth is, marketing, like any other profession, requires years of study, research, and experience. Yet, **we've all encountered those executives or colleagues in other departments who vastly oversimplify marketing** and **feel compelled to share their "expert" opinion.**

- "Our product is so good, it'll sell itself. The product team can handle the messaging."
- "We need a press release on this, right now."
- "Let's make more videos and go viral."
- "Have you seen the competitor's weekly newsletter? Let's throw one out too."
- "We're not on TikTok, we must be missing out."

Over time, you get used to these types of comments. **But what truly empowers you to seamlessly handle them is having a solid plan. It's what helped me flip the dynamic.**

With a well-thought-out strategy, you can confidently respond, acknowledging their input while steering the conversation back to the strategy at hand. A robust plan allows you to focus on what matters and communicate why certain suggestions might not align with current objectives. This becomes especially important when dealing with feedback from leadership or board members.

Marketing plans need to be designed and built, with simplicity, purpose, visuality, and creativity. I hope the structure, ideas, and templates to follow **provide inspiration for you and help you to create your own …**

Indigo Blueprint
to drive B2B product marketing success.

2

Build a Solid Foundation

 If you begin with the basics by looking at the fundamental definitions of marketing and product marketing, **the list of what you could be, and (should be?) doing is practically limitless.**

Marketing, they say, is the process of creating, communicating, delivering, and exchanging offerings that have value for customers, clients, partners - and society as a whole. It involves finding customer needs and wants, developing products or services that satisfy those needs, promoting and selling those products or services, and building relationships with customers to ensure their continued satisfaction and loyalty.

Marketing encompasses a wide range of activities, including market research, product development, advertising, public relations, sales, customer service, and more. Its ultimate goal is to attract and retain customers, and to generate profitable revenue for the company or organization.

Product marketing is commonly defined as a branch of marketing that focuses on the promotion and positioning of a specific solution, product, or service. It involves understanding the target audience and developing strategies to promote the features, benefits, and unique selling points of a particular product or service.

Product marketing includes activities such as market research, competitive analysis, product development, pricing, packaging, distribution, and promotion. It also involves working closely with other departments within the company, such as sales, engineering, and customer support, to ensure that the product meets the needs of the target market and is properly positioned in the marketplace.

The ultimate goal of product marketing is to drive sales and revenue growth by creating awareness and demand for the product or service among the target audience. Effective product marketing strategies can help a company differentiate its product from competitors, increase brand loyalty, and build long-term customer relationships.

Together, the sheer scope of possible paths and tasks presents an overwhelming number of scenarios. This is further complicated by a blurring of roles between marketing and product marketing ownership as to who is truly responsible for what.

It's at this intersection that three guiding principles emerge which allow leaders and teams to take a step back, and communicate how to work together towards the same objective. As the foundational pillars of a solid plan, these principles provide a framework for cohesive collaboration. The aim is to instill clarity and purpose, bringing the collective focus onto a single shared goal.

This is where the importance of an organized plan begins. It is where the most successful product marketers think like a CMO, a Chief Marketing Officer, in how they approach their position.

#1: Do Three Things with One Objective

The first guiding principle is about simplifying what all marketing activities should aspire to do. Despite the complexity, they should aspire to do one of three things. They should work to build awareness, generate demand (and leads), or enable sales. The ultimate objective is then only one especially important thing. That's to drive revenue for the business. Revenue may be from the sale of products and services, or in the case of a start-up, revenue may be from the sale of the company. But driving revenue is always the goal.

This is where the plan starts, its framework. Simply put, **it is what marketing, and product marketing, does. Align your plan to address each of the three critical elements.** They then connect, working together to drive a focused and measurable impact to the business.

What all marketing activity should aspire to do

Build awareness → Generate demand → Enable sales

$ **Drive revenue**

Build Awareness

Building awareness involves creating visibility, recognition, and familiarity with the brand and its offerings among the target market. Both brand awareness and solution awareness are crucial for marketing success. They are also quite different. Brand awareness helps to establish credibility, trust, and recognition for the brand. If there is one topic that's been covered extensively in marketing resources, and rightly so, it's brand. My favorite is a textbook classic called *Strategic Brand Management* by Alexander Chernev. It lays out a comprehensive and organized approach to understanding the key principles of building enduring brands. For product marketing teams, the focus rests more with solution awareness. That's ensuring that the target audience understands the specific solutions or products that the brand offers and their relevance to their needs or pain points. If a customer has bought from you, they've become aware of your brand. There's really no need to measure brand awareness anymore. Unless you're doing Pepsi commercials. Which is only a handful of companies.

Generate Demand

In marketing, **demand generation and lead generation** are two distinct but closely related concepts. While both are focused on driving business growth, they target distinct stages of the customer journey and employ different strategies. Demand generation is the process of getting people interested in what a company has to offer (creating demand); lead generation is the task of turning that interest into names and contact details (leads) that marketing and the sales teams can follow up with. Sometimes it gets confusing, so here's a straightforward breakdown of the differences.

Demand generation refers to activities aimed at creating awareness, interest, and demand for a company's products or services among a broader target audience. It focuses on generating demand from potential customers who may not be actively searching for a specific solution. The goal of demand generation is to educate and engage the audience, nurturing them into becoming interested prospects.

Demand generation takes prospects all the way from establishing their awareness that they have a problem the company can help them solve, through increasing trust and confidence in the company's brand, to definite interest in what solutions can do for them. It might include raising awareness of product features and why they matter, sharing thought leadership content that demonstrates industry expertise, distributing free resources that show how useful the company and its products and services can be, or sharing influencer posts from leadership that showcase a company's brand or core values.

Key aspects of demand generation include:

- **Content marketing**: Creating and distributing valuable, informative, and engaging content to attract and engage the target audience.
- **Thought leadership**: Establishing the brand as an industry authority and expert through thought-provoking content, speaking engagements, or expert opinions.
- **Public relations (PR) and social media**: Using PR efforts and social media platforms to generate buzz and attention around the brand and its offerings.

The aim of demand generation is to create a positive perception, generate interest, and ultimately drive potential customers to enter the sales funnel as leads.

Lead generation translates the interest that all this activity creates into something tangible and actionable. It focuses on finding and attracting potential customers who have expressed an explicit interest in a company's products or services. It involves capturing their contact information, typically in exchange for valuable content or an offer, and converting them into leads. The goal is to gather qualified leads that have a higher likelihood of converting into paying customers.

Key aspects of lead generation include:

- **Landing pages and lead capture forms**: Creating dedicated landing pages and forms that capture contact information in exchange for content or offers.
- **Lead magnets**: Offering valuable resources, such as eBooks, whitepapers, webinars, or free trials, to entice potential customers to provide their contact details.
- **Email marketing and nurturing**: Engaging with leads through targeted email campaigns to build relationships, educate them further, and guide them through the buying process.
- **Lead scoring and qualification**: Assessing leads based on their level of engagement and how well they fit with the target customer profile to prioritize sales efforts.
- Lead generation **focuses on moving potential customers from initial interest to a more direct sales conversation** and is centered around identifying individuals who are likely to convert into customers.

While demand generation creates interest in a broader audience, lead generation is more focused on converting interested prospects into qualified leads that can be pursued by the sales team. Both strategies are crucial for marketing success and should be interconnected in a comprehensive marketing campaign.

Enable Sales

In the B2B world, sales enablement refers to the process of providing sales teams with the resources, tools, information, and support they need to effectively engage with potential customers, close deals, and drive revenue growth. It aims to equip sales professionals with the necessary knowledge, skills, and assets to engage buyers at every stage of the sales cycle.

Sales enablement encompasses various activities and strategies, including:

- **Content creation**: Developing sales collateral, presentations, case studies, product sheets, and other relevant materials that align with the buyer's journey and address customer pain points.
- **Training and education**: Providing sales teams with ongoing training and education to enhance their product knowledge, sales techniques, objection handling, and understanding of the target market.
- **Sales tools and technology**: Equipping sales teams with tools and technologies such as customer relationship management (CRM) systems, sales automation software, sales intelligence platforms, and analytics tools to streamline their processes and improve productivity.
- **Sales process optimization**: Defining and refining the sales process, including lead management, pipeline management, and sales methodologies, to ensure efficiency and effectiveness.
- **Collaboration and communication**: Facilitating collaboration and knowledge sharing among sales teams, marketing teams, and other departments to align efforts and enhance overall sales effectiveness.

It's important to note, however, that sales enablement is an area typically picked up by various departments. This can include marketing and product marketing, but also sales, product management, training departments, sales operations teams, marketing operations teams, or customer support teams. **Misalignment of what sales enablement is at your company, and who owns which aspects can result in conflicts and misunderstandings between teams about definition, responsibility, budgets, and goals.** For example, marketing may be focused on content development, marketing ops may be working with sales ops to concentrate on managing the sales process and tracking outcomes, while product management may be solely responsible for product training.

At a minimum, marketing's priority should first be on sales content optimization. Does the sales team have the content they need and is it well organized in an easy to access location? Equally important, do they have support for customization needs?

> Contrary to common belief,
> marketers are not the only ones creating content.

In fact, many salespeople are busy creating copious amounts of content in the form of custom PowerPoint presentations. And it's fair to say, most of them are not very good, with marketing teams unwilling to help.

There is an excellent book that was given to me called *slide:ology: The Art and Science of Creating Great Presentations* by Nancy Duarte. She talks about how "few things could be more anticlimactic than a massive marketing campaign followed by an unorganized, unmoving presentation ... (that) may be the last engagement you have with your customers before they make a purchase decision."[2] Profound words of wisdom to remember. **Every customer deserves a great presentation.**

It's likely well understood, but remember that sales enablement is crucial for several reasons:

- **Enhanced buyer experiences**: With proper sales enablement, sales teams are better equipped to understand customer needs, provide relevant information, and deliver a personalized buying

---

[2] Nancy Duarte, *slide:ology The Art and Science of Creating Great Presentations* (O'Reilly Media, 2008), p. 4.

experience. This helps build trust and credibility, ultimately improving the overall customer experience.
- **Consistent messaging and brand representation**: Sales enablement ensures that sales teams have access to up-to-date and consistent messaging, positioning, and branding. This consistency in messaging across the organization helps reinforce the brand and build a cohesive customer experience.
- **Alignment between sales and marketing**: Effective sales enablement fosters alignment and collaboration between sales and marketing teams. It ensures that both teams are working together towards shared goals and objectives, and that marketing efforts are tailored to support sales activities.
- **Empowering sales teams**: Sales enablement provides sales professionals with the resources and knowledge necessary to engage with customers effectively. It helps them address customer pain points, manage objections, and show the value of the products or services they offer.
- **Increased sales productivity and efficiency**: By providing sales teams with the right tools, technology, and processes, sales enablement streamlines their workflows, reduces administrative tasks, and enables them to focus more on selling. This results in increased productivity and efficiency.

Bottom line, sales enablement plays a vital role in driving effectiveness, improving customer experiences, and boosting revenue in the B2B world. It's a bridge between your marketing success and sales excellence – don't overlook it.

Drive Revenue

Although various marketing activities are designed to produce results at different stages of the buyers' journey, they all ultimately support one primary goal: revenue. **That's why it's**

crucial to learn how to keep score. Figure out how to do it within your company and work to put your revenue impact into your marketing plan from the start. Being solid on focused metrics does two things:

- Allows you to make decisions on what worked and what didn't, and
- Helps you prove your value to the business.

Demonstrating a clear impact on revenue and return-on-investment (ROI) is vital for marketing teams because it provides a direct link between their marketing efforts and business outcomes. It aligns marketing with the overall business objectives and is vitally important for several crucial reasons:

- **Business growth and sustainability**: Ultimately, the primary goal of marketing is to drive business growth and generate revenue. A marketing strategy that effectively impacts revenue helps a company thrive, expand its market share, and achieve long-term sustainability.
- **Resource allocation**: Marketing budgets are limited, and organizations need to allocate their resources wisely to get the maximum return. Demonstrating a positive impact on revenue and ROI allows marketers to justify their budget requests and secure necessary funds to execute strategic initiatives.
- **Decision making and strategy refinement**: Measuring the impact of marketing efforts on revenue and ROI offers valuable insights into the effectiveness of different marketing campaigns, channels, and tactics. This data-driven approach allows marketing teams to make informed decisions, optimize strategies, and focus resources on activities that deliver the best results.

- **Accountability and performance evaluation:** Demonstrating the impact on revenue and ROI holds marketing teams accountable for their efforts. By quantifying the results, companies can evaluate the performance of their marketing initiatives and identify areas for improvement.
- **Credibility and buy-in:** Proving the positive impact on revenue and ROI enhances the credibility of the marketing team within the organization. It also encourages buy-in and support from other departments and stakeholders, fostering a collaborative environment focused on achieving business objectives.
- **Competitive advantage:** Effective marketing strategies that drive revenue growth can help a company gain a competitive advantage. With a strong ROI, a company can outpace competitors in reaching target audiences, capturing market share, and sustaining growth.
- **Business valuation:** For investors and potential partners, a company's marketing performance and its impact on revenue and ROI are critical indicators of its financial health and growth potential. Strong marketing results can positively influence business valuation and attract investment opportunities.

A great place to start is always:

- Where you are today,
- Where you want to be (your vision and goals), and
- What's in your way (pay attention to any obstacles).

Industry benchmarks are a nice point of reference, but what are your numbers doing today, and what are you doing to make them better tomorrow?

#2: Know Your Audience, Value and Voice

The second guiding principle is about staying grounded in the basics. Working closely with sales to understand the customer, working closely with the product team to understand the value proposition, and working closely with corporate marketing to shape the right positioning and message.

Know your **audience**	Know your **value**	Know your **voice**
Sync with sales	**Align with product**	**Unite with brand**
Understand needs and pain points, profile and segmentation, buyer personas and journey	Articulate why a product is special; convey the value it adds in the customer's own language	Shape a clear, compelling message; assure the story is well told and aligned across touchpoints

 Be the central connection

Do you understand your audience, know your product or service appeal and differentiation? Is it a difference that the market is willing to pay for? Are you able to communicate the products' values in a clear and compelling way?

While it seems elementary, I believe a majority of B2B companies can't succinctly and clearly answer these questions.

Despite the importance of this, many B2B companies struggle with it. Some of the reasons why it can be challenging for them are understandable:

- **Complexity of B2B products and services**: B2B offerings can be complex and involve multiple

stakeholders in the decision-making process. Communicating the value proposition effectively in such scenarios can be challenging.
- **Internal silos**: In some companies, different departments may have varying perspectives on the target audience and value proposition, leading to inconsistent messaging.
- **Technical jargon**: B2B companies may use technical language and industry jargon that can be confusing to their target audience. Communicating in a more accessible and customer-centric manner can be difficult.
- **Lack of clarity**: Companies may have a general idea of their value proposition, but they struggle to articulate it concisely and convincingly.
- **Fear of commitment**: Some companies may be hesitant to focus on a specific audience or value proposition, fearing it might limit their potential market.
- **Timing pressure**: At times, there can be a strong push to enter an emerging market before a company knows enough about the audience and the value a product brings. This pressure often stems from the business's need to demonstrate growth for shareholders, leading to premature market entry.

As a result, unfortunately, the challenge of articulating good value propositions often looms large, and the answer becomes a common pitfall. It is the reliance on the solitary expert for solutions that are "so complex that only certain individuals can speak to them properly." This luminary figure, be it the product manager, or typically an executive, **becomes the sole custodian of a product's narrative**. However, this narrative, when tethered to a lone voice, becomes unsustainable and lacks scalability. More crucially, it does a disservice to the product and the business. Imagine a scenario where only a select group of "subject matter experts" hold the keys to effectively communicating the virtues of a product. It's a set-up that echoes frustrations in creating marketing messages and lacks any type of scalability.

Yet despite these difficulties, there lies an opportunity for product marketers. It's a chance to change the dynamic; to be the positive catalyst at the intersection of marketing and product teams, driving forth a wave of clear communication and collaboration. It begins with your audience.

Know Your Audience

Defining your target audience is a fundamental step in creating a focused and effective marketing strategy. The goal is to create a detailed and nuanced profile of the ideal client, the specific group of people that you want to reach and engage with, to effectively communicate with your marketing.

Certainly, a lot can be said about target markets and audiences, in addition to various segmentation strategies and methodologies for approaching buyer mappings. But the first step is a common denominator in using various means to effectively uncover who they are, including market research, data analytics, feedback loops, and industry trends. Of course, not all companies or teams have the resources to cover all possible sources. But do your best to explore and access as many options as practical.

- **Surveys and questionnaires**: Direct feedback from your audience through surveys helps gather quantitative and qualitative data.
- **Competitor analysis**: Studying competitors can reveal insights into shared target audiences and strategies that work in your industry.
- **Customer interviews**: Conducting one-on-one interviews with existing customers and potential prospects provides qualitative insights into their needs, challenges, and preferences.

- **Website analytics**: Analyzing website data can reveal information about your current audience, their behavior, and preferences.
- **Social media analytics**: Insights from social media platforms provide data on audience demographics, engagement, and content preferences.
- **Customer feedback**: Actively seek and analyze customer feedback, whether through surveys, reviews, or direct interactions. This ongoing feedback loop helps adjust strategies based on real-time insights.
- **Collaboration with sales**: Sales teams often have direct interactions with customers. Collaborate closely with the sales team to gather their input and insights into customer conversations, objections, and preferences.
- **Staying informed**: Regularly reviewing industry reports, trends, and market analyses. Understanding the broader industry context can help refine your understanding of your target customers.

To craft a comprehensive profile of your target audience and construct a buyer persona, you'll delve into three key dimensions: firmographics, demographics, and psychographics.

Buyer personas

For both Strategic Sam and Tactical Tim

Firmographic data
- Industries, sectors, named companies, look-alike accounts

Demographic insights
- Job description, age, income level, education, location (rural, urban, suburban)
- Interests, favorite blogs, and news sources

Psychographic knowledge
- Challenges and goals
- Values and fears
- What they might expect from us
- Common concerns that prevent them from converting

It's not just about who they are and what they do but also about why they make the decisions that they make. This comprehensive understanding is invaluable for tailoring marketing efforts that truly connect with your audience on a personal and meaningful level.

Let's explore these three facets in greater detail:

- **Firmographic data and identifying companies**: This involves pinpointing the specific industries or sectors that your company aims to serve. Additionally, it entails determining the ideal size of businesses that align with your offerings. Within firmographics, you establish a list of named accounts—specific companies you target—and identify look-alike accounts that share similar characteristics with your ideal customers.
- **Demographic data for executive and practitioner audiences**: Demographic data such as population, race, income, education, and employment are bifurcated into two critical segments: Strategic Sam (representing your executive-level audience) and Tactical Tim (representing your practitioner-level audience). Both segments play pivotal roles in closing B2B deals, yet they may have distinct messaging needs. Crafting tailored messages for Strategic Sam and Tactical Tim is crucial, recognizing that their roles, responsibilities, and decision-making processes differ significantly. This personalization enhances the effectiveness of communication strategies.
- **Psychographic data in understanding wants, needs, and fears**: Psychographic data delves into the emotional and psychological aspects that influence customer decisions. This involves understanding the wants, needs, and fears of your target audience. Psychographics pay attention to the audience's perceptions, thoughts, and beliefs. It explores the

deeper motivations and values that guide their decision-making, offering insights into how your product or service aligns with their worldview.

In essence, this holistic approach to audience profiling enables a nuanced understanding of the diverse factors that shape your target customers.

By combining firmographic insights about the companies you target, demographic details about the people involved, and psychographic understandings of their motivations, you equip your strategy with the depth needed to resonate effectively.

Understanding your target audience goes beyond the who, what and why of your buyer personas; it also involves comprehending "how" your product or service addresses customers' problems, wants, and needs.

> Use cases, often overlooked, are pivotal narratives that really belong upfront in your marketing plan, intricately woven with your target audience profiles.

Use cases
Create a headline that captures a benefit

Challenge
- Describe the key customer challenge in context of their need and application.

Solution
- Articulate how you solve a customer challenge; how the solution addresses it.

Impact
- Show the expected benefit and any unique advantages in helping them achieve their goal.

What image best captures the use case visually?

These stories unfold logically, starting with the customer's challenge, introducing the solution, and concluding with positive outcomes.

They provide a real-world context, bridging the gap between theoretical features and practical business challenges.

When crafting use cases, specificity is paramount. For a Chief Financial Officer (CFO), a use case might spotlight financial benefits, while one tailored for an IT manager could emphasize security features. Infusing quotes and testimonials lends an authentic voice, making experiences relatable to others. Quantifying impact, whether in terms of increased efficiency, cost savings, or revenue growth, adds compelling substance. Visual elements, such as charts or before-and-after visuals, enhance the storytelling, making complex information more digestible.

In essence, use cases are more than marketing collateral; they are strategic assets that articulate the tangible value of your offerings in a language that resonates with your target audience.

Remember, knowing your target customer is not a one-time activity. It's an ongoing process that evolves as market dynamics change. Regularly reassessing your understanding of your audience ensures that your marketing strategies stay relevant and effective.

One of my favorite reminders about avoiding oversimplification of a target audience has been around for several years, and I'm glad to see it recirculating recently through multiple LinkedIn posts.

It describes two individuals: both male, born in 1948, and raised in the U.K. Both have been married twice, live in castles, are wealthy, successful in business, and like dogs. They seem to have quite a lot in common. Or do they? When you realize that the two individuals are King Charles and Ozzy Osbourne, it becomes quite clear that you would likely market to each of them very differently.

Know Your Value

Crafting a compelling value proposition is not just a task; it's a strategic imperative that demands solid attention.

Value proposition

What is your product; what does it do?	Succinctly answer
Who are your targets; segments, companies, orgs?	
What problem does your product solve?	
How is it different from competitors?	
How will it benefit your customers?	
What is its unique value?	
What key features does it include?	

 We help (x) do (y) by doing (z), delivering (a, b and c) benefits, and unlike the competition, we uniquely do (this) distinctly better to meet market needs.

In its simplest terms, a value proposition is a positioning statement that explains what benefit you provide for who and how you do it uniquely well. It describes your target buyer, the pain point you solve, and why you're distinctly better than the alternatives. It explains how your product's benefits and features meet and exceed your customer's wants, needs, and fears – and the experience it delivers.

One often overlooked crucial aspect of the value prop is the statement "unlike the competition, we uniquely do this or that." **Competitive strategy and differentiation** are complex topics for executive leadership and product management teams to address well *before* the product marketing team is asked to articulate it. Too many times though, I've experienced a lack of either. But that's not to say that it's easy to determine and build. It can be challenging for several reasons:

- **Increasing globalization**: The marketplace is more globalized than ever, and companies often run in a highly interconnected world. This can make it challenging to find and maintain unique differentiators as competitors from different regions may offer comparable products or services.

- **Technological convergence**: Rapid advancements in technology have led to the convergence of features and functionalities across various products and solutions. What was once a unique feature may become a standard offering in the industry, making it difficult to stand out.
- **Short product lifecycles**: The speed at which products and technologies evolve has shortened product lifecycles. This means that what may be a unique selling point today could become obsolete or commonplace in a truly short amount of time.
- **Mature markets**: In mature industries, products and services may have similar features, making it challenging to find truly distinctive points of differentiation. Customers may view offerings as commodities, leading to a sole focus on price competition.
- **Customer expectations**: With increasing customer expectations, companies often need to meet a baseline of features and functionalities just to stay competitive. This can make it hard to differentiate based solely on product features.

It's important not to rely on the usual talking points that many brands default to, such as promoting innovation, claiming to be a trusted advisor, offering custom-designed solutions, integration, one-stop shopping, enhancing efficiency, and driving business success. Even if the presentation looks impressive, your solutions often end up looking remarkably like those of your competitors and many other companies.

Most B2B tech companies operate in a very crowded competitive space. Collaboration among leadership, product, engineering, marketing, and sales teams is essential to identify your true differentiation from a customer perspective. Once identified, articulate it simply and make it a core part of your value proposition. Potential differentiators can encompass a wide range of possibilities:

- **Product differentiators**: Putting a focus on value, not just features. Product differentiation is the unique characteristics and capabilities of your product — its features and benefits, design, user experience, quality, and performance. Don't allow yourself or teams to get caught up in dwelling on lengthy detailed comparisons by features and specifications. It's a path to commoditization and allows the buyer to focus on price comparison and reduction. Rather than solely relying on features, emphasize the overall value your product or solution brings to the customer. This includes factors such as improved efficiency, cost savings, and positive business outcomes.
- **Customer-centric differentiation**: Understanding your customers deeply, including their pain points and specific needs. Tailoring your offerings and services to address these unique customer challenges, creating a differentiated and personalized customer experience.
- **Innovation**: Investing in ongoing research and development (R&D) to stay ahead of industry trends. Innovation can lead to the creation of new features or solutions that set your product apart.
- **Brand differentiators**: Cultivating a strong brand and reputation in the market. How your customers recognize, perceive, and relate to your brand. The advertising that you do can play a significant role in creating a positive brand association for your audience. A positive brand image can differentiate your company even when product features are similar.

- **Customer service and support:** Service differentiators can be the unique ways that your company creates a relationship with customers. Every interaction a prospect or buyer has with a representative of the business is important - such as customer service calls, support emails, live chat help, and exchanges on social media. Exceptional customer service can be a powerful differentiator. Providing excellent support, training, and after-sales service can build strong customer loyalty.
- **Strategic partnerships:** Collaborating with other companies or forming strategic partnerships that enhance your offering. Integrating with complementary solutions can provide added value to customers.
- **Niche targeting:** Identifying niche markets or specific industry segments where your product can uniquely meet specialized needs. Being a specialist in a particular area can lead to strong differentiation.
- **Sustainable practices:** Considering environmental and ethical factors in your business practices. Sustainability and responsible business conduct can be a unique selling point, especially in markets where these considerations are valued.
- **Price differentiators:** Price differentiators refer to how you structure the pricing of your offering, including the amount charged and the frequency of payment collection from customers. Pricing models can also serve as differentiators by simplifying the purchasing experience. For example, offering a bundled solution at a single price versus individually pricing software and hardware components can reduce friction for the customer. Or if your business operates at a premium level, clearly communicating the added value justifying the higher price (such as

unique software capabilities or superior customer support) can serve as distinctive attributes.
- **Channel differentiators**: Channel differentiators refer to the ways your company gets its offering to customers. These include how your product is distributed and where it is sold.

> "The competitor to be feared is the one who never bothers about you at all – but goes on making his own business better all the time." - Henry Ford

In summary, competitive differentiation requires a strategic approach that goes way beyond product features. By focusing on delivering value, understanding customer needs, and innovating in ways that align with market trends, B2B companies can successfully stand out in today's competitive landscape.

Know Your Voice

Once you have a deep understanding of your audience and a clear articulation of your value proposition, developing **a messaging framework is the commitment to consistency** across communication channels. It serves as a guide for aligning communication efforts across various channels and touchpoints.

A well-developed messaging framework should ensure that your marketing messages are cohesive, resonate with your audience, effectively convey the value proposition of your product or service, and are in alignment with your brand values. While the beginning template may seem simple at first, developing a creative and effective framework can be much harder than it appears. But by following some best practices, you can craft a reference guide that serves as an extremely helpful tool.

Messaging framework

Elevator pitch			
Messaging pillars	Key message #1	Key message #2	Key message #3
Customer pain points	Define issue or opportunity		
Supporting points and key capabilities			
Customer benefits	Advantage #1 Advantage #2 Advantage #3		
Keywords			

- **Draft your positioning statement and brief narrative in the form of an elevator pitch.** You need to catch your audience with a concise description of a product or solution that explains its value in a way that any listener can understand. You can't afford to be boring or confusing, but need to deliver a short, sweet, and irresistibly compelling spiel that leaves your audience eager for more. In the world of elevator pitches, brevity is the key to opening doors, closing deals, and leaving a lasting impression. The average elevator pitch ranges from 20-30 seconds, but you should offer multiple options. A good rule of thumb is to have three.
    - A short pitch at 20 words
    - A medium pitch at 40 words
    - A long pitch at 60-80 words
- **Create a messaging hierarchy**: Underneath your elevator pitch belongs a hierarchy of messages, with the most critical and impactful messages at the top. This helps ensure that your core messages receive the emphasis they deserve and are consistently communicated across different channels.
- **Address pain points**: Your messaging should be based on problem-solution alignment and should

directly address the pain points of your audience. Clearly communicate how your product or service provides a solution to their challenges, making their lives better or easier.

- **Keep a consistent tone and style**: Maintain a consistent tone and style throughout your messaging. Whether it's on your website, social media, or marketing collateral, a uniform voice builds brand recognition and trust.
- **Use stage-relevant messaging**: As you can expand and build out a more robust hierarchy, tailor your messages to various stages of the customer journey. Early-stage messages may focus on awareness, while later stages might emphasize specific features or benefits.
- **Utilize storytelling and narrative elements**: Incorporate storytelling elements into your messaging. Stories resonate with audiences and make your messages more memorable. If possible, connect each messaging element to one of your use cases to add a human touch.
- **Address objections**: Anticipate common objections or concerns that your audience might have and address them proactively in your messaging. This builds credibility and helps overcome potential barriers to conversion. The sales team will thank you for taking the time to work this through.
- **Train teams and gain internal alignment**: The framework value extends well beyond the marketing team's use. It's vital to ensure that your entire team, from marketing to sales, is aligned with the messaging framework. Conduct training sessions to familiarize team members with key messages, ensuring consistency in external communications.
- **Adapt and update as needed**: The market always evolves, and so should your messaging framework.

Regularly revisit and update your messaging to align with changes in the industry, competitive landscape, or customer preferences.

The last core element of the framework is figuring out your keywords. Keywords play a pivotal role in marketing across various channels, and their importance stems from their ability to connect businesses with their target audience effectively. Why are they so critical in marketing?

- **Search Engine Optimization (SEO) and discoverability:** Keywords are fundamental to SEO, where they help search engines understand the content of web pages. By optimizing content with relevant keywords, businesses increase their chances of being discovered by users searching for related products, services, or information.
- **Search Engine Marketing (SEM) and ad relevance:** In paid advertising campaigns, selecting the right keywords ensures that your ads are displayed to a relevant audience. The choice of keywords directly influences the ad's visibility and its alignment with user search queries.
- **Content marketing relevance and engagement:** Keywords guide content creation by ensuring that the material aligns with what users are searching for. Relevant keywords enhance the visibility of content, leading to increased organic traffic and engagement.
- **Social media marketing targeting and reach:** On social media platforms, using keywords in posts, captions, and hashtags helps in targeting specific audiences and expanding the reach of content. This is particularly relevant for platforms like Instagram and X.
- **Understanding customer intent:** The choice of keywords reflects user intent. Understanding the keywords users are using provides valuable insights

into what they are looking for and helps businesses align their messaging with customer needs.
- **Monitoring competitors**: Analyzing competitor keywords allows businesses to understand their competitors' strategies, identify gaps, and refine their own keyword selection to maintain competitiveness.
- **Brand visibility**: Consistent use of branded keywords helps establish and reinforce a brand's online presence. When users search for a specific brand or related products/services, optimized use of keywords enhances visibility.
- **Performance tracking**: Keywords are integral to tracking the performance of marketing efforts. By analyzing keyword performance metrics, businesses can measure the effectiveness of their strategies and make data-driven decisions for optimization.
- **Product discoverability**: In e-commerce, keywords are crucial for product listings. Properly optimized product titles, descriptions, and tags help improve the discoverability of products in online marketplaces.

Keywords serve as the bridge between businesses and their target audience in the vast online landscape. Whether in SEO, SEM, content marketing, or other channels, the strategic use of keywords ensures that marketing efforts are aligned with customer intent, leading to increased visibility, engagement, and, ultimately, conversions. Regular keyword research, analysis, and optimization are essential components of a dynamic and effective marketing strategy.

#3: Understand the Strategic Priorities

The third guiding principle is about the importance of understanding strategic priorities. Business, marketing, and go-to-market … it all starts with a strategy. And if you have the wrong one, or you don't have one at all, the rest really doesn't matter.

> *"Knowing what to leave out is just as important as knowing what to focus on." - Warren Buffett*

So, what's the secret to success? There is no one secret to modern marketing success, as the field of marketing is constantly evolving and **the strategies that work best will vary depending on the industry, target audience, and other factors**. However, there are certain key principles and best practices that help companies achieve success in their marketing efforts:

- **Customer focus**: Successful modern marketing puts the customer at the center of everything. Companies must understand their customers' needs, preferences, and behaviors to create products, services, and marketing campaigns that resonate with them. It sounds so simple, yet many times, companies get so caught up on internal issues that they lose focus on the customer.
- **Data-driven decision-making**: With the abundance of data available in today's digital world, it's essential for companies to use data to inform their marketing strategies. This means tracking and analyzing customer data to gain insights into their behavior and preferences, as well as measuring the effectiveness of marketing campaigns and making data-driven decisions based on the results. Be mindful though, an overload of data analysis can paralyze a team, hindering decision-making and stalling progress.
- **Agility and adaptability**: Modern marketing requires the ability to quickly adapt to changing trends and consumer behavior. Companies must be able to pivot their strategies as needed to stay ahead of the curve and meet their customers' evolving needs.

- **Integration and alignment**: Successful modern marketing requires alignment across all aspects of the organization, including sales, product development, customer service, and more. This means creating a cohesive brand message and experience across all channels and touchpoints and ensuring that all departments are working together toward common goals.
- **Innovation and creativity**: Finally, successful modern marketing requires a willingness to take risks and try new things. Companies that are willing to experiment with innovative technologies, platforms, and strategies are more likely to stand out in a crowded marketplace and capture the attention of their target audience.

But most importantly, your marketing strategy should begin by simply aligning with the company's business objectives. It can then serve as your guide to making informed decisions and allocating resources efficiently. And it will clearly illustrate how your approach is in direct support of the larger organization's goals, so that everyone understands the connection and impact.

Know the business objectives. Whether your marketing efforts are supporting a solitary product within a portfolio, or you have ownership of the company's overarching product marketing plans – it's vital to look at the big picture – whether it's your place within a larger context, or all in together. At large companies, this view can sometimes be extremely challenging to decipher and simplify.

What are the bookings targets? By business unit, by portfolio, and by product? What is the revenue breakdown by region or segment/vertical as applicable? What percentage of revenue comes from the top x customers? Has the business unit clearly shown their top five priorities? For example, are they defending market leadership under attack, expanding into new adjacent markets, or diversifying with new products in new areas of growth?

Articulate the strategic priorities. Only after the business objectives are clearly understood can you begin to lay out a viewpoint of strategic marketing priorities. At an early-stage start-up, there may be only one product to bring to market. But in most established B2B companies, the portfolio (and competing objectives) can be quite extensive. In this case, the marketing team can tremendously help an organization move from numerous individual product-focused strategies to a more unified approach – products and services viewed working together at the customer level.

The template to follow is one example of how to map out focus and flow.

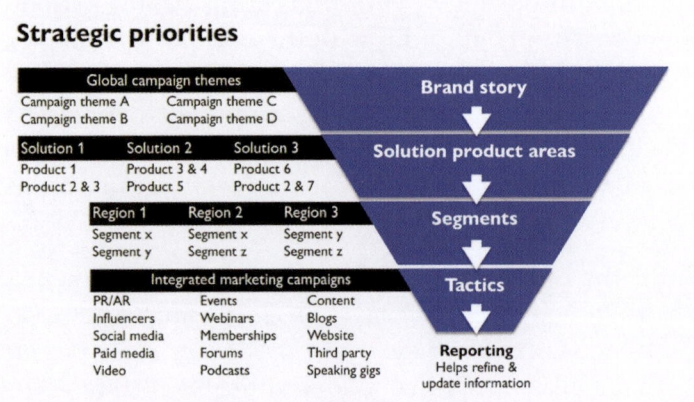

It begins with the company's global campaign themes. Typically, it's one to three "umbrella" topics, commonly focused on the most relevant technology use cases that customers and prospects are facing.

A global campaign theme refers to a central, unifying concept or idea that serves as the foundation for a marketing campaign launched across multiple solutions and regions. It's the overarching message or story that ties together all the various components of the campaign—advertisements, content, visuals, and messaging—across diverse markets. Key characteristics of a global campaign theme include:

- **Consistency**: The theme ensures a consistent message is communicated across all regions, providing a cohesive brand experience. This consistency helps in building a unified brand identity worldwide.
- **Adaptability**: While the core theme stays consistent, it allows for adaptation to local cultures, languages, and market nuances. This ensures that the campaign resonates with diverse audiences.
- **Alignment with brand values**: The theme typically aligns with the brand's core values and objectives. It reinforces the brand's identity and positions it in a way that is meaningful and relevant globally.
- **Scalability**: The theme should be scalable to accommodate variations in market sizes, cultural sensitivities, and regional preferences. It should be broad enough to encompass diverse contexts.
- **Memorability**: A successful global campaign theme is memorable and leaves an impression on the audience. It captures attention and has the potential to become synonymous with the brand.
- **Cross-channel integration**: The theme extends across various marketing channels, including digital, print, social media, and events. This integration ensures a comprehensive and cohesive brand presence.

Developing a global campaign theme involves strategic thinking and a deep understanding of the target audience. It's a delicate balance between creating a unified global brand image and recognizing the unique characteristics of individual markets. As a product marketer, how does your product align with global campaigns so you can best leverage?

The next layer is in many ways, telling of how well a company has rationalized and optimized their portfolio. In lieu of a lengthy list of products, what are the **key solution areas** that can support multiple product offerings, and which are the priority to the business? Focusing marketing campaigns and spending on these key solution areas can help streamline budgets and resources to improve overall efficiency. As a product marketer, how does your product align with key solution areas so you can best leverage?

The third layer is about the sales organization's priorities. By region or country, where are the priorities in segments? Once again, it is not asking for an extensive list but working to find a focus on key drivers for the business, the priorities.

Only after the business has clearly communicated the top three layers, should the fourth layer come into play. It is then that the integrated marketing campaigns can be designed and built. Reporting is then focused on these key areas, as opposed to being lost in too many detailed metrics. The metrics can also then help refine and adjust the strategy itself going forward. What's working, what's not.

Strategy is defined as a general plan to achieve one or more overall long-term goals under conditions of uncertainty. Conversely, tactics refer to the specific set of actions taken to reach the organizational goals, or strategy.

> Many times, there's a tendency to confuse strategy with tactics. The tendency is to jump straight to the tactics.

Taking the time to understand and communicate back to the business the strategic priorities is an important first step.

Traditionally, **a marketing strategy** is your comprehensive plan and set of actions designed to achieve specific marketing objectives and goals. It serves as a roadmap that guides an organization's marketing efforts to reach and engage its target audience effectively, differentiate its offerings from competitors, and ultimately drive business growth and success. A well-developed marketing strategy typically includes:

- **Market analysis**: Assessing the target market, including customer demographics, behaviors, needs, and preferences. This involves conducting market research, analyzing industry trends, and evaluating the competitive landscape.
- **Target audience segmentation**: Identifying distinct customer segments within the broader market based on factors such as demographics, psychographics, buying behaviors, or specific needs. This helps in tailoring marketing messages and tactics to resonate with each segment.
- **Value proposition**: Defining and articulating the unique value and benefits that a product or service offers to customers. This involves understanding the competitive advantages, key differentiators, and the positioning of the brand in the market.
- **Marketing objectives and goals**: Establishing clear and measurable objectives that align with the overall business goals. Objectives can include increasing market share, revenue growth, brand awareness, customer acquisition, or customer retention.
- **Marketing mix**: Developing a strategic combination of marketing tactics and channels to reach the target audience effectively. This includes decisions on product/service offerings, pricing, distribution channels, and promotion (advertising, public relations, digital marketing, social media, content marketing, etc.).
- **Implementation plan**: Outlining the specific action steps, timelines, responsibilities, and budget allocation needed to execute the marketing strategy effectively.

This ensures that the strategy is implemented in a coordinated and consistent manner.

- **Measurement and evaluation:** Defining key performance indicators (KPIs) and metrics to track the effectiveness and success of the marketing efforts. Regular evaluation allows for adjustments and refinements to optimize the strategy and achieve better results.

A go-to-market strategy is then a subset of the overall marketing strategy. It is specific to the introduction of something new, such as the launch of new products or expansion into new markets. While a marketing strategy is a longer-term, broader plan for the organization, a go-to-market strategy is usually the overarching framework that guides how a company will bring its products to market. More on that is covered in Chapter 5.

3

Create a Repeatable Framework

With a solid foundation in play, the next layer is to create a repeatable campaign framework. Successful marketing campaigns can be tremendously complex. They are a multi-faceted orchestra that craves content. Lots and lots of content. Especially in B2B technology markets with highly advanced technical solutions. In addition, campaigns can be an unruly arena where everyone seems to hold a perspective on what they should entail. For me, having a repeatable campaign framework became not just a strategy, but a lifeline in taming the potential pandemonium.

This is where the concept of **"marchitecture"** comes into play - a fusion of **mar**keting and a**rchitecture** that emphasizes the strategic design and construction of comprehensive marketing frameworks. Just as an architect meticulously plans and designs a building, a **"marchitect"** is someone who specializes in the art and science of creating these marketing frameworks.

I was first introduced to the concept by my colleague, Peter Schorsch – a well-respected B2B marketing leader and resourceful trailblazer. **Not only is Peter an incredibly talented marchitect, but he has also significantly shaped my understanding of how to build and implement these frameworks effectively.** His expertise has deepened my appreciation for the meticulous planning and creative insight required to excel in this field.

A skilled B2B marchitect, like Peter, has the unique talent of seeing the bigger picture while paying attention to the finer details, ensuring that every campaign is not only well-planned but also aligned with overarching business goals. They excel in integrating various marketing elements - such as messaging, content, channels, and performance metrics - into a cohesive structure that drives results.

In addition, a marchitect is both creative and analytical, capable of designing a framework that is flexible enough to adapt to changing market conditions while being robust enough to deliver consistent performance. They bring together different facets of marketing into a unified strategy, ensuring that every campaign is built on a solid foundation that can scale and evolve with the business.

It is this approach and expertise that we'll delve into here. So where does it all begin? It starts with alignment - both within your organization's campaign framework and across the customer journey.

Align Campaigns and Content

Working together, it's important for marketing organizations to first structure and coordinate the various types of B2B campaigns typically found. Basically, there should be three types of key campaigns: global corporate campaigns, product campaigns and field marketing campaigns (sometime referred to as regional or channel/partner campaigns).

> When siloed, they can cause a tremendous amount of confusion to sales and customers.
>
> When coordinated, they can deliver significant and noticeable value.

Create a Repeatable Framework

- **Global campaigns**, as mentioned previously, are well-coordinated in planning and primarily concentrated on awareness and demand generation, the top half of the funnel. They are typically based on broader themes that cover the most relevant technology use cases or key solution areas that customers and prospects are facing. They may target different market segments globally, and a company may have one or multiple global campaigns running. They are always on and long-term in length, meaning they can be active for eight to twelve months or longer. While the content and tactics will change throughout the year, the overarching umbrella message remains steady and consistent. If marketing budgets are limited, global campaigns can take advantage of account-specific targeting using marketing technology that can specifically target the accounts a company cares about most.
- **Product campaigns** are more focused, product-centric, and time-limited campaigns primarily for major launches, releases, and promotions. This area is expanded upon further in Chapter 5.
- **Regional campaigns** (or sometimes called field or channel campaigns) are in-English or local language campaigns designed to meet more specialized region or partner-specific objectives.

As a product marketer, it's important to make sure you are leveraging the complete framework.

That you are championing your products into global campaigns providing the necessary support, that you are also initiating a series of successful product campaigns, and that you are connected to the field marketing and sales teams to assure your products are active and visible in their more localized regional efforts. Ideally, all three areas work together towards the same goal.

Once your campaign framework is understood and aligned, it's key to determine **the content needed to fuel your campaigns – and to align that content within the customer buying cycle and sales funnel**. Although a buyer's journey is anything but linear, and certainly much more complex than a few stages, I have found it helpful to view content alignment along three primary categories: education, solution, and selection. It keeps the structure simple, without overthinking.

Align content development to customer buying cycle

	Education		Solution		Selection	
Objective	Create interest and position ourselves as able to offer relevant insight and advice		Build engagement with the customer and shape their thinking around the value of our solutions		Convert the prospect's interest into an intent to purchase our solution and overcome any concerns	
Help the customer understand what?	Thought leadership	Solution awareness	Value story	Solution advantage	Financial reasoning	Decision validation
Assets						
Tactics						

- **Education:** Typically, is the content aligned to the top of the funnel. Its aim is to create interest which

starts a buying journey and positions a company's ability to offer relevant insight and advice. It is the home for thought leadership assets and tactics, in addition to broader solution-based content.
- **Solution:** Commonly positioned with the middle of the funnel. It's designed to build engagement with the customer and shape their thinking around the value of products and solutions. This area of content focuses on the value story and a product or solution's differentiation.
- **Selection:** Aligned with the bottom of the funnel, its purpose is to convert the prospect's interest into an intent to buy a product or solution and overcome any objections or concerns. This is where financial justification and decision validation pieces come into play.

It's at this point that a content audit can be an invaluable exercise. Yes, a content audit of all existing content. You may be surprised at what you find. It's an interesting exercise to look at the full library by content type, by product or solution area, by buyer stage, and by buyer type. How does your current content support key campaign needs, and how does it align to the journey? Where are there gaps to fill and where are new opportunities to refresh or build out your library? The content audit allows you to:

- Identify what content is missing.
- Discover what content is underperforming. Which pieces of content aren't getting the numbers you want.
- Locate content that is outdated. If you have old content, determine if you can update or rework it. If not, retire it as it only becomes clutter.
- Identify your top content. Which content is your best performer?

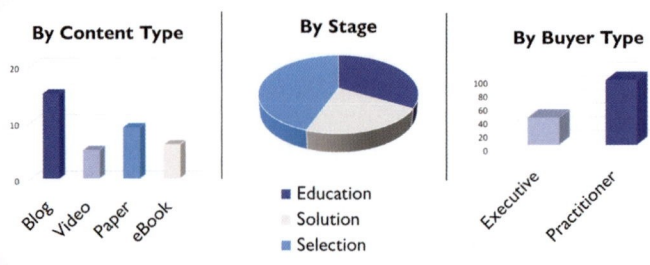

Although a content audit can take some effort (whether you complete it in-house or outsource to an agency), it should be telling of a clear path forward. Where you may have too much content, not enough content, are covered well or need new, etc. It's all about helping to find the right balance to best tell your story.

Craft a Story That Resonates

Crafting a story doesn't mean you need to make something up. In fact, the best place to start is simply with the truth. From there, you can capture, build, and shape your narrative. It becomes your unifying theme, the anchor, that all your related content flows from. It embodies your brand values. It supports your value proposition.

It should be told from a customer perspective, in a way that is authentic and human, helpful and engaging. Think of it as communicating person-to-person (P2P) as opposed to business-to-business (B2B). It can be technically knowledgeable and informative, but never condescending. B2B customers are smart. More times than not, they are equally (or if not more) savvy in the technology or business areas of interest.

When creating your marketing story, it's interesting to consider **who typically provides the initial input.** It often comes from two extremes. On one side, senior management wants to drive the narrative, resulting in PowerPoint presentations filled with bullet points. While this format is easier for the presenter, it often lacks substance and detail, making it challenging for marketing and the audience. It avoids crafting a coherent story that can be easily remembered and repeated. Writing out a pitch, explanation, or idea in complete sentences to tell a full story is much harder but forces deeper clarity.

On the other side, product experts within a company want to drive the narrative, resulting in content that is much too technical. This type of material may be suited for specific types of content for practitioner-level audiences, but the strong technical bias usually makes it exceedingly difficult, if not impossible, to allow it to work for most of the marketing content.

Additionally, different audiences require information to be pitched differently, and different sources of content require marketing to gather, edit and shape it in different ways. So, what's the solution? I've found that the best approach is to capture and curate.

> "Sometimes reality is too complex. Stories give it form." - Jean Luc Godard

Capturing the viewpoints of different perspectives, from leadership, to product, to engineering, to sales, support teams, and customers can provide a much more insightful and well-rounded story. After all, content creation is not solely the responsibility of the marketing department. Everyone should be contributing to the story that they are a part of, the company, the solutions, the challenges, the success.

A good B2B copywriter can help with gathering input from these resources. They bring a unique set of skills that go beyond just writing – including the ability to interview your content sources and capture their insights from a more natural conversation perspective. They understand the nuances of B2B transactions, articulating value, and driving meaningful engagement with a target audience. They are part storyteller, strategist, and communicator rolled into one. It is worth the investment to partner with the right B2B copywriter that is a good fit for your brand, type of product, style, and team.

Once your writer has completed interviews and gathered any other written reference materials – the organization and presentation of a story will emerge and flow much more easily.

Curating is defined as an endeavor of selecting, organizing, and presenting to give the information an artistic form that adds interest, ease of understanding, and value.

Investing the time to curate a full-featured piece of rich content *that presents your complete story*, delivers a hero for your campaign. As the **"cornerstone"** asset, it is typically some type of long-form content, such as an e-Book or report that seamlessly incorporates the mix of perspectives. For example, it may include market insights, helpful data, customer quotes, both executive and practitioner insights, infographics, etc.

From there, you can easily adapt the content to various shorter forms to create a multitude of **"cobblestone"** content pieces (such as blogs, articles, social posts, and more), adjusting the messaging to suit each format, maximizing its effectiveness. The key to cobblestone content is striving to produce high-quality content that answers more specific questions buyers may have as they move through the buying process. It should be the best answer to a question people ask along the journey of your story.

A great exercise is to brainstorm a list of the different questions your customers might ask about the problem your product or service solves. You can use a great tool like AnswerThePublic.com to help you. It generates questions based on specific words, such as who, what, when, and where. These questions can provide insight into what people are asking about a particular topic, which can help with your content creation.

Cobblestone content can also cover adjustments for versioning, whether for specific regions or channels, or audience types – from practitioner to executive. Always strive to make your cobblestone content relevant, interesting, timely – and visually appealing. And at times, if appropriate, entertaining.

> Having a foundation in place, an audit complete, and your story defined, can help steer you to which content will work best.

As you create your content plan, it's helpful to think about how you can curate the right collection of content for your audience. That includes how you structure its discovery, making it as easy as possible for the prospects you are trying to cultivate. Technically, there's only four types of content to choose from. That is written, visual, audio and video. But that would be too easy. Truthfully, the list of possible assets is numerous and diverse. It can be unrealistic (and quite overwhelming, not to mention budget-busting) to plan for continuously creating them all.

The following is a list of the diverse types of marketing content to consider in your mix. Content development takes time and money, and a content plan is a must have. Leveraging the cornerstone/cobblestone approach and mapping the right content to your campaign needs and journey, is a smart move to help you stay focused and organized.

- **Blogs and articles:** Informative and engaging written content published on a website.
- **Infographics:** Visual representations of information or data, combining images and text.
- **Social media posts:** Content shared on social media platforms, including text, images, and videos.
- **Paid advertisements:** Search and display ads for relevant platforms (including re-targeting ads and multiple versions).
- **Videos:** Visual content that can include product demos, tutorials, testimonials, FAQ shorts and more.
- **Podcasts:** Audio content that can cover assorted topics and be shared through platforms like Spotify or Apple Podcasts.
- **eBooks:** Longer-form content often used for in-depth exploration of a topic.
- **Whitepapers, reports, or guides:** In-depth assets that offer valuable insights or solutions.
- **Case studies:** Detailed examinations of specific projects or success stories.
- **Webinars:** Online seminars or workshops delivered through the web.
- **Email campaigns:** Targeted messages sent to a list of subscribers.
- **Interactive content:** Content that allows users to engage actively, such as quizzes, polls, or interactive graphics.
- **User-Generated Content (UGC):** Content created by users, such as customer reviews, testimonials, or social media posts.

Create a Repeatable Framework

- **Newsletters**: Regularly distributed updates, often via email, holding news, offers, or valuable content.
- **Slide decks**: Presentations created using slides, often shared on platforms like SlideShare.
- **Lists**: Top 10 list articles, known as 'listicles', which answer questions or provide interesting information and data.
- **Product literature**: Solution briefs and technical specifications.
- **GIFs and memes**: Short, animated images or humorous content used for engagement.
- **Surveys and polls**: Interactive content that gathers feedback from the audience.
- **Live streaming**: Real-time video broadcasts on platforms like Facebook Live or Instagram Live.
- **Visual quotes and graphics**: Images containing inspirational or informative text.
- **Interactive maps**: Maps that users can interact with, providing information on locations.
- **Augmented Reality (AR) and Virtual Reality (VR) content**: Immersive experiences that leverage AR or VR technologies.

As you build quality content, remember to build "findable" quality content. Search engine optimization (SEO) is more important than ever as B2B buyers continue to conduct extensive research online before making decisions. Your resource skilled in SEO (whether that is your copywriter, an agency resource, or in-house specialist) can help you create content that not only engages the audience but also ranks well on search engines, increasing the business's online visibility. SEO is an ongoing process, not a one-time strategy. You need to continually work at it, in partnership with your content, to see the best results.

Thankfully, technological innovation has brought us help. As a marketer, having lived the constant pressure to produce a steady stream of growing content needs, I was quite welcoming of the new advancements in AI. Quite honestly, it was mesmerizing. I didn't view it as a replacement for marketing teams or writers, but as an amazing new capability that could make content creation easier, faster, and better. From my perspective, the significant value it brings is a game changer.

- **Timesaving**: AI tools can help automate time-consuming tasks such as research and content generation. This can help content creators to focus on the creative aspects of their work, thereby increasing their productivity and efficiency.
- **Personalization**: AI-powered content creation can be personalized to suit individual preferences and needs. This can help marketers to create more targeted and effective marketing campaigns, bloggers to tailor their content to their audience's interests, and authors to cater to their readers' preferences.
- **Quality**: AI can help to improve the quality of content by suggesting improvements, finding errors, and providing feedback on readability, tone, and style.
- **Creativity**: AI can aid content creators in generating new ideas and concepts by analyzing data, identifying patterns, and suggesting new approaches. This can help to inspire new and innovative content ideas.
- **Scalability**: With the help of AI, content creation can be scaled to meet the demands of a larger audience. This means that businesses can produce more content without sacrificing quality or efficiency, helping to drive greater engagement and conversions.

It's important to note that the effectiveness of content depends on factors like audience preferences, the context of use, and the overall marketing strategy. Regularly assessing performance through analytics and adapting content strategies accordingly is key to sustained success.

According to the Content Marketing Institute, only 28% of B2B marketers say their organization is extremely or very successful with content marketing.

These top performers most often attribute their success to knowing their audience (79%). Among other factors are having content that aligns with the organization's objectives (68%), effectively measuring and demonstrating content performance (61%), thought leadership (60%), collaboration with other teams (55%), and documented strategy (53%).[3]

> You'll no doubt be judged by your content.
> It's an area to invest in.

Integrate Your Marketing Tactics

Once you have employed the right mix and range of content types, it's then time to employ the right mix and range of tactics to get your message (and content) out to your targeted accounts.

Integrated marketing campaign tactics typically span three primary areas: digital (covering both web and platforms), influencer relations (also covering analyst and press relations), and events.

---

[3] 'Content Marketing Stats You Should Know', by Lisa Murton Beets, Content Marketing Institute, published November 29, 2023, https://contentmarketinginstitute.com/articles/content-marketing-statistics.

Integrated marketing campaigns tactics

- Digital marketing campaigns
- Influencer relations incl. AR-PR
- Field marketing events

Employ the right mix

Digital Marketing Campaigns

The digital marketing campaign is your **organized series of online activities and efforts designed to achieve your objectives**. It involves the use of various digital channels and platforms to reach and engage a target audience, promote your products or services, and ultimately drive desired actions, typically awareness and conversions. Choosing the digital channels and platforms that are most effective for reaching your target audience may include your social media, search engines, email, several types of content marketing, display advertising, and more.

New marketing mediums will continually emerge, and that's okay. My advice is to embrace change - and then focus on the channels that will best support your plan. Managing too many channels at once can be tough, so avoid spreading yourself too thin. Choose the channels that align with your target audience, while considering your budget and the type of content you're creating. A marketing engine delivers the best results for your solutions when you develop "full funnel" content that supports multiple tactics across the buyer's journey. Below is an example of how to map these needs effectively.

Create a Repeatable Framework

Delivering content to target accounts
Employ a wide range of content types and digital tactics to get your message out

TACTICAL ASSETS	eBook	Report	Blog	Paper	Video	Case study	Infographic	Webinar
Gated asset landing page	x	x		x				
Paid media landing page	x	x		x				
Event landing page								x
Resource library page	x	x	x	x	x	x	x	x
Display advertising	x	x						
Paid social – LinkedIn	x	x						
Paid social – X	x	x						
Retargeting	x	x	x	x				
Paid search	x	x		x				x
Social (organic)	x	x	x	x	x	x	x	x
Content syndication	x	x			x	x	x	
Email nurture	x	x	x	x	x	x	x	x
Sales email-invite								x

(Digital Marketing Campaigns)

Digital campaigns usually run on one of three main media channels. Each type has distinct characteristics, and they each play distinct roles in a comprehensive marketing approach.

- **Owned media.** Such as your mailing lists, websites, and social accounts.
- **Paid media.** Including search engine advertising and sponsorships.
- **Earned media.** Such as external PR placements and network marketing.

Owned media refers to the channels and platforms that a company or brand controls and manages. These are the digital or physical assets owned by the business. Examples include: your company website, blogs, social media pages, email newsletters, print materials, etc.

- **Characteristics**: The content is entirely controlled by you. It provides full creative control over messaging and branding and is directly managed and maintained by the business. It offers a platform for brand storytelling, product showcases, and information dissemination.
- **Purpose**: Owned media serves as a foundation for a brand's online presence. It provides a controlled

environment for sharing information, building brand identity, and engaging with the audience directly.

Paid media involves promotional activities for which a company pays a fee to reach a specific audience. It includes advertising placements on external platforms or media channels. Examples include display ads, Pay-Per-Click (PPC) advertising, social media ads, sponsored content, influencer marketing (when payment is involved), etc.

- **Characteristics**: It requires financial investment but provides immediate visibility and reach. Message placement is determined by the payment made and is often used for targeted campaigns to reach specific demographics.
- **Purpose**: Paid media is employed to amplify reach, drive traffic, and promote specific campaigns or products. It is a strategic way to increase brand visibility quickly.

Earned media refers to publicity or exposure gained through organic means, where the audience and media voluntarily share or talk about a brand without direct payment. Examples include media coverage (news articles, TV features), social media mentions and shares, customer reviews and testimonials, word-of-mouth referrals, viral content, etc.

- **Characteristics**: It's not directly paid for or controlled by the brand. It relies on positive interactions and experiences that lead to organic mentions. Word-of-mouth and social sharing contribute to its growth. It's reputation-driven and often seen as more authentic.
- **Purpose**: Earned media reflects a brand's reputation and the quality of its products or services. Positive earned media can enhance credibility and trust.

Create a Repeatable Framework

Integration in a media strategy is essential. An effective media strategy often involves a combination of owned, paid, and earned media. They work synergistically to create a comprehensive and well-rounded approach to marketing.

> **Paid** media can amplify the reach of **owned** media, while positive **earned** media can positively influence paid media performance.

Understanding the distinctions between owned, paid, and earned media is crucial for businesses to develop a holistic media strategy that effectively reaches, engages, and influences their target audience. The key is to create a cohesive and well-coordinated effort. The following visual is one such example of a campaign framework designed to maximize lead production.

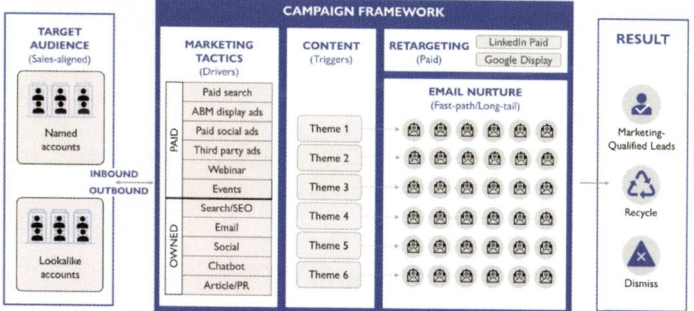

As you design your own integrated digital marketing campaign plan, it can be helpful to view it as a four-step process.

Step One: Be realistic.

An effective plan hinges on execution, a process tightly dependent upon your available resources - be it the talent within your team, the tools at your disposal, or the financial investment you're willing to make. It starts with an introspective examination. Do you have the right personnel equipped with the necessary skillsets? This might span from a proficient marketing operations team adept at systems and data analysis to skilled content writers, graphic designers, web developers, SEO experts, and beyond.

From a tool perspective, do you have a strong technological infrastructure, a well-built tech stack that aligns with your objectives? Imagine trying a social campaign without the existence of a managed social media profile or planning an email outreach initiative with a non-existent or subpar contact list. The choices in the landscape of marketing platforms and tools are numerous and vast – so likely vary greatly by company.

Lastly, the temporal and financial dimensions are critical. Do you have the luxury of time or is time a luxury you do not have? Is your budget aligned with the ambitions of your digital marketing endeavors? Do you have a clear view of costs and pricing? These questions lay the groundwork for a plan that is not just aspirational but also realistic, considering the practicalities that can make or break the success of your digital marketing initiatives.

Ahead in Chapter 6, you'll find additional thoughts on the right team, tools, and budget.

Step Two: Use your foundation.

We've already touched on the fundamental basics. The time invested in them will have helped set you up for success - as they become the core of your campaign.

- ✓ **Clear objectives:** Clearly define the goals of the campaign in support of building awareness and generating demand to drive revenue. Make sure they are aligned to business priorities and objectives.

- ✓ **Well-understood account targets**: This information along with audience profiles guides the customization of marketing messages and strategies to resonate with the intended audience.
- ✓ **Compelling messaging**: Crafting a consistent and persuasive message that communicates the value proposition and key benefits of the product or service. The messaging should be tailored to resonate with the target audience.
- ✓ **Solid content plan with quality assets**: Developing compelling and relevant content to be distributed across chosen digital channels to tell your story. Content may include blog posts, articles, images, videos, infographics, and other formats that align with the campaign objectives. It includes advertisements and social post creation for the selected digital channels and platforms.

Step Three: Select your channels.

The third step is about choosing the digital channels and platforms that are most effective for reaching your target audience. This most commonly includes:

- **Your company website** is a primary hub for all digital marketing and sales activity. It is the centralized platform for showcasing your products, services, and brand identity. If your company has invested well in its website, keeping it modern, refreshed, and dynamic – then congratulations. Your job is so much easier. Either way though, as a product marketer, it's vital to make sure you invest your time and effort in your product's representation, pages, and content. The website is the digital face of your product, offering comprehensive information and acting as a conversion powerhouse. It's the primary destination for building credibility and trust. How does your web presence look and perform? Are you optimizing its potential?

- **The corporate blog** is a dynamic space for in-depth content, an opportunity to educate, engage, and build a narrative around your product. It's a tool for thought leadership and industry expertise and can also provide a forum for more in-depth and technical topics. A blog can include content formats like listicles, how-tos, product reviews, and so much more. Blogs can help establish authority, driving organic traffic and fostering a community. They provide valuable insights, address pain points, and keep the audience informed.
- **Search.** Search Engine Optimization (SEO) enhances organic visibility, while paid search (PPC) ensures immediate visibility through targeted advertisements on search engines. SEO boosts long-term visibility, and paid search provides instant results. Together, they cover both organic and immediate search needs.
- **Social media** platforms offer a dynamic space for product communications. Organic efforts involve regular posts, while paid strategies amplify reach through targeted ads. Social media is where audiences can actively engage. We love it for its immediacy, shareability, and sense of community. Typically for B2B, LinkedIn and X lead the way as the most popular, relevant, and effective platforms. But that's not to say your business may not also benefit from a profile on Facebook, TikTok, Instagram or other platforms. It's simply a great deal of work that goes into posts and ad creative for social sites to deliver and capture attention in such crowded spaces. So, it may be a better strategy to do a select number of platforms extremely well, before overextending a team.

Create a Repeatable Framework

- **Display advertising** uses visual elements to capture attention on websites, apps, or social media. They come in various formats, including banners, images, and videos. Display ads are visually impactful, capturing attention swiftly. They are effective for brand awareness, retargeting, and driving specific actions.
- **Re-targeting**, also known as remarketing, is a digital advertising strategy that involves displaying targeted ads to individuals who have previously interacted with a brand's website, content, or products. It works by tracking users' online behavior, such as visiting specific pages or engaging with certain content, and then presenting them with relevant ads across various platforms. Re-targeting addresses the reality that not all website visitors convert on their first visit and recognizes that decision-making processes in B2B can be lengthy, requiring multiple touchpoints before a prospect commits. Moreover, re-targeting enables advertisers to deliver personalized content based on users' earlier interactions. This level of customization ensures that the ads presented align closely with the prospect's interests, needs, or pain points. The result is a more relevant and engaging advertising experience.
- **Email marketing** involves sending targeted messages to a subscriber list. It nurtures leads, shares valuable content, and promotes products or services. Email is a direct line to your audience. It's chosen for its personalization, automation capabilities, and high potential for conversion.
- **Video marketing**, whether short video clips or longer narratives, engages and entertains. It's shared on platforms like YouTube, social media, and company websites. You may choose to share your video content on landing pages, or on a co-

marketer's website. Video is captivating and versatile. It's chosen for its storytelling ability, the potential for virality, and its effectiveness across various platforms.

- **Webinars** are online seminars or workshops. Sponsored webinars involve partnering with experts or influencers to share insights with your audience. Webinars can provide in-depth education, position you as an industry leader, and offer direct interaction with the audience, building trust and authority.

Don't forget to master your gateway. Marketing landing pages are the standalone web pages created specifically for your campaigns. They are the heart of your marketing funnel and often overlooked. Their primary purpose is to convert visitors into leads or customers by encouraging a single specific action, such as filling out a form, downloading a resource, making a purchase, or subscribing to a service. Unlike regular web pages, landing pages are designed with a singular focus on a particular call-to-action (CTA), eliminating distractions to increase the likelihood of conversion. A well-designed landing page guides visitors toward a specific conversion goal, seamlessly tailored to match the content and messaging of the campaign. Best practices in their creation may be well understood, but a checklist is always of benefit.

- Craft a headline that clearly communicates the value proposition and **grabs the visitor's attention at once**.
- Keep the messaging concise and focused on the specific offer or campaign. **Avoid unnecessary information that may distract visitors**.
- Use **high-quality and relevant visuals**, such as images or videos, to enhance the visual appeal of the landing page and support the message.

- Place **a prominent and compelling call-to-action (CTA)** that clearly instructs visitors on the next step. Make the CTA button visually distinct.
- If the goal is to collect information through a form, keep it short and only ask for **essential details**. Use strategic form placements.
- Ensure that the landing page is **optimized for mobile devices**, as a sizable portion of users may access it from smartphones or tablets.
- Maintain **consistent** branding elements, including colors, fonts, and logo, to reinforce brand identity and trust.
- Write persuasive and **benefit-driven copy** that clearly communicates the value of the offer and addresses the visitor's pain points or needs.
- Include testimonials, reviews, or trust badges to build **credibility** and reassure visitors about the legitimacy of the offer.
- **Conduct A/B testing** to experiment with different elements on the landing page, such as headlines, visuals, or CTAs, to optimize for the best conversion rates.

By adhering to best practices, marketers can create landing pages that not only align with their campaign objectives but also provide a positive and effective user experience, ultimately driving desired actions from their target audience.

Step Four: Run and manage your campaigns.

Running and managing your campaigns may be quite different dependent upon the size of your company and the structure and capabilities of your marketing team. The role of a Marketing Operations (MOPs) manager and digital campaign team (in brevity) is to help oversee the execution and management of marketing campaigns – including measuring performance and support for data-driven decision making. The reality is that their role is essential for running effective campaigns, especially at scale. But for purposes here, the final aspects of your plan address the following.

- **Implementation**: Executing the campaign activities across chosen digital channels. This involves scheduling content, launching advertisements, and managing interactions with the audience.
- **Budget management**: Effectively allocating and managing the budget for the digital marketing campaign. This includes figuring out the right spending levels for each channel and optimizing the budget based on performance.
- **Monitoring and analytics**: Regularly watching the performance of the campaign using analytics tools. Tracking key performance indicators (KPIs) helps assess the effectiveness of each channel and the campaign, allowing for adjustments based on real-time data.
- **Optimization**: Analyzing the campaign's performance data and making strategic adjustments to optimize its effectiveness. This could involve refining targeting parameters, adjusting advertising spend, or tweaking content based on audience feedback.
- **Conversion tracking**: Implementing mechanisms to track and measure conversions, whether they are sales, sign-ups, downloads, or other desired actions. This helps assess the ROI and the overall success of the campaign.

The awesome thing about digital marketing channels is there's no one correct way to reach your audience.

Do your homework, experiment, and watch results to zoom in on what engages your audience. Above all, do your best to deliver value. If your marketing helps customers learn, solve a problem, gain an advantage, or just smile a little – you're likely to be on the right track.

Influencer Relations

Over the last 20 years, the role of Public Relations (PR) in marketing has undergone significant transformation. It has evolved to take on a larger role under the more prominent umbrella of 'Influencer Relations.' This includes Public Relations, Analyst Relations (AR), Industry Organizations and of course Influencer Marketing. Influencer Relations (IR) professionals now navigate a dynamic, digital, complex landscape, leveraging technology, social media, and integrated strategies to engage audiences, and adapt to the ever-changing dynamics of the modern marketing environment.

The boundaries between traditional PR and marketing have blurred, leading to more integrated approaches. PR is often seen as an integral part of overall marketing strategies with its own unique challenges.

- **Real-time communication and speed of response**: The rise of digital platforms has accelerated the pace of communication. PR professionals now engage in real-time communication, responding to news and trends as they unfold on social media and other online platforms. PR efforts use social platforms to build relationships, manage reputations and disseminate information. The speed at which information spreads in the digital age necessitates rapid crisis response strategies. PR professionals now need to address and manage crises swiftly to control narratives and mitigate reputational damage. The 24/7 news cycle demands continuous communication. PR professionals need to be agile in responding to news, trends, and events happening across the world.
- **Influencer marketing**: The emergence of influencers has become a significant aspect of PR. Collaborating

with influencers allows brands to reach niche audiences through trusted personalities. They are often experts and thought leaders that boast a dedicated online following, lending credibility to your message.
- **Multichannel distribution**: PR professionals now have access to a multitude of channels to distribute content. This includes owned media (company websites), earned media (traditional and online publications), shared media (social platforms), and paid media (content promotion).
- **Global reach**: The digital landscape has facilitated global PR campaigns. Brands can now reach international audiences, and PR strategies often consider cultural nuances and regional preferences.
- **Data-driven decision making**: The availability of data analytics tools has enabled PR professionals to measure the impact of their efforts more accurately. Metrics such as website traffic, social media engagement, and sentiment analysis provide insights into campaign effectiveness.

Whether your IR-AR-PR team is in-house or via agency (or ideally both), it's time well spent for product marketers to collaborate closely with them to build out a specific plan of action that coordinates in support of your digital marketing campaign. It may include:

- Upcoming **media announcements** related to your product.
- Aid with scouting the right **influencer(s)** and ideation on how to creatively engage them. Figure out (then leverage) why it is that people love and follow them.
- List of top **industry analysts** most relevant to your product, including strategy on how to best build a relationship with and leverage.

Create a Repeatable Framework

- Key **industry forums or technology organizations** that the company is currently a member of (or those it should be), along with plans on how to maximize exposure.
- **Noteworthy industry awards** you can submit nominations for.
- The **speaking engagements** you would like to solicit to build thought leadership in your space.
- **Articles to present for earned media placement**, and a list of which media outlets and target publications to pursue.
- **Media training** for any team members interested in supporting your product's voice in public forums.

Field Marketing Events

In B2B marketing, field marketing events refer to in-person initiatives that take place outside of the office or headquarters, often with the goal of engaging directly with target customers, generating leads, and building relationships. These events can include trade shows, conferences, seminars, workshops, roadshows, and various other face-to-face interactions with potential clients and industry professionals.

In my travels, I've experienced success at some truly amazing events. As example, the Consumer Electronics Show in Las Vegas every January, and Mobile World Congress in Barcelona, Spain every February. The energy and excitement can be incredibly motivating. On the other end, I've also experienced great success at very small, more intimate events in the shape of customer roadshows, seminars, and dinners. Yet an endless debate over the value of events always seems to be present. A debate within organizations whether a company should continue to fund and support events, or not. With sales and product teams pushing for more events, and marketing and finance pushing for less, it's been useful more than once to step back and present the pros and cons.

The pros of field marketing events are many.

- **Networking opportunities**: Events provide a platform for networking with potential clients, partners, and industry experts, fostering valuable connections.
- **Visibility**: Participation in industry events enhances brand visibility and awareness within the target audience.
- **Product demonstrations**: Hands on. Real. Events provide an opportunity to showcase and demonstrate products or services in a live setting, allowing potential clients to experience them firsthand.
- **Education and thought leadership**: Hosting or participating in workshops and seminars allows companies to position themselves as thought leaders and educate the audience about industry trends and best practices.
- **Face-to-face communication**: Direct interactions facilitate in-depth conversations, allowing businesses to understand customer needs and concerns on a personal level.
- **Market research**: Events offer a chance to gather feedback, observe competitor activities, and conduct informal market research.
- **Relationship building**: Face-to-face interactions contribute to relationship building, which is crucial for long-term B2B partnerships.
- **Lead generation**: Yes, lead generation. Field events offer a chance to capture leads through interactions and engagement, leading to potential business opportunities. I would not select events as the primary driver for leads, nor lead generation as the primary reason for doing events. However, it's worth mentioning as in some markets, industries, and circumstances, it can remain a tangible benefit.

And yet the cons of field marketing events are many, too.

- **Costs**: Field events can be expensive in terms of booth space, travel, accommodation, marketing collateral, and other related expenses.
- **Resource intensive**: Planning and executing successful events requires considerable time and resources, including labor, logistics, and coordination.
- **Limited reach**: Field events may have a limited audience compared to digital marketing efforts, which can reach a broader geographic scope.
- **Variable ROI**: The return-on-investment (ROI) from events can be variable, and it may be challenging to directly attribute business outcomes to specific events.
- **Dependency on external factors**: The success of an event may be influenced by external factors such as the overall attendance, industry trends, or the economic climate.
- **Logistical challenges**: Managing logistics, including travel arrangements, booth setup, and event coordination, can pose challenges.

In the ever-evolving landscape of B2B marketing, I believe that field marketing events continue to adapt to technological advancements and changing preferences to remain effective and impactful for businesses. The best approach is to lay forward a plan. Which events are selected and why, along with the expected participation, cost, and results. Then communicate it broadly - so the plan and calendar are clear.

> **If your prospects and customers are still attending events, do events. If they are not, don't.**

Spotlight the Meaningful Metrics

Having solid marketing metrics is vital, yet they can be ridiculously complex spanning diverse platforms, systems, product lines, and campaigns. It's no secret that we as marketers continually grapple with multiple challenges in acquiring and reporting on them. The challenges to follow are the big ones. And their accompanying solutions are major platform investments and initiatives (time, money, and talented resources) that may or may not be in place, depending upon the company.

- **Data accuracy and integration**: Ensuring the accuracy of data seems to be a persistent challenge. Data may come from various sources, and integrating it into a cohesive, accurate dataset can be taxing. Solution: Investing in robust data integration tools and regularly auditing data sources can help enhance accuracy.
- **Attribution modeling**: Determining the contribution of each marketing channel to conversions is a complex task. Attribution models often face challenges in accurately assigning value to touchpoints. Solution: Employing advanced attribution models and using multi-touch attribution tools can provide a more nuanced understanding of channel contributions.
- **Cross-channel measurement**: Marketing occurs across various channels, both online and offline. Measuring and attributing success across these channels can be intricate. Solution: Implementing cross-channel measurement tools and analytics platforms helps in understanding the holistic impact of marketing efforts.
- **Privacy concerns and compliance**: With increasing emphasis on privacy regulations, collecting and using customer data responsibly becomes challenging.

Solution: Ensuring compliance with data protection laws, such as GDPR or CCPA, and adopting privacy-conscious analytics practices is essential.
- **Measuring customer experience**: Quantifying the impact of marketing on overall customer experience can be challenging. Solution: Implementing customer experience metrics alongside traditional marketing metrics provides a more comprehensive view.

However, the purpose of this conversation is not to delve into the mechanics of various platforms nor recommendations. But I felt it was important to first acknowledge and respect just how vast and sophisticated data and systems can be. Getting a strong engine in place is not a light lift.

The focus here is to present how to approach what metrics you may want to zero in on. For example, **how can you more confidently discuss with your leadership and marketing operations team which metrics you need and why?** To avoid getting lost in the vortex of endless details you could pursue, it can be extremely useful to first outline your framework and organize the important objectives in a simplified manner.

Begin by setting up clear and measurable objectives that align with the overall business goals. As said earlier in Chapter 1, the ultimate objective is typically only one particularly important thing. That's to drive revenue for the business. But your objectives may also include important sub-targets such as increasing market share, acquiring new customers or retaining existing customers. Stay focused when determining your objectives. The less objectives you have, the more focused you can be on driving success.

It's then important to define your key performance indicators (KPIs) and the more specific metrics required to track the effectiveness and success of your marketing efforts. It can be useful to think about as three primary objectives:

- **Performance**: To help measure and communicate marketing's impact and do a better job of justifying the importance of marketing investments.
- **Optimization**: To facilitate decisions and optimize marketing's contribution to the business while being most efficient with your spending and resources.
- **Cost-Effectiveness**: To understand the cost effectiveness of your marketing spend.

As you dive in, step back and think about what you are trying to affect, the impact on the business. For example, when thinking about demand generation, there's only two levers to pull.

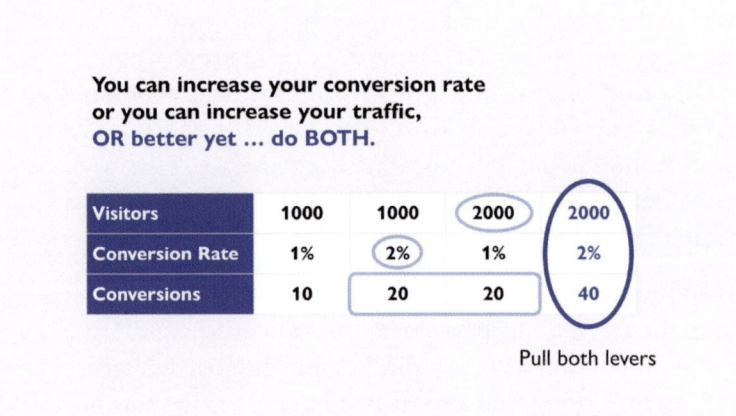

Pull both levers

Get more people to see your stuff or get more people to convert. How do you drive more demand for your product? Pull both.

> The point is, the more you can simplify your metrics "story" – the easier and more impactful it is to communicate to leadership and across the organization.

A Scorecard for Performance. An optimal marketing scorecard for executives should include key metrics that provide a concise and meaningful overview of the marketing team's performance and its impact on the organization's goals. The scorecard should focus on both quantitative and qualitative data that align with business objectives and are easily digestible for executives. Here are some essential key metrics to consider:

- **Pipeline performance:** Marketing-qualified leads (MQLs), sales-qualified leads (SQLs) and sales opportunities – along with conversion rates, and the sales pipeline amount that they generated (in dollars). This is the number of leads that marketing has identified as qualified and handed over to the sales team, in addition to the sales opportunities those leads resulted in, including the number of opportunities and dollar value of those opportunities. This should also include a Leads by Source view. These metrics demonstrate the quality of leads generated by marketing and where they originated.
- **Revenue impact:** The overall revenue generated as a direct result of marketing efforts, in addition to the overall revenue generated as an indirect result of marketing efforts, meaning was influenced by marketing efforts. This metric shows how marketing contributes to the company's financial success.
- **Website and content performance:** Number of users, new vs. returning, traffic and device sources, conversion rate, average search position, in addition to pageviews, top viewed pages, average session duration and bounce rate. This also may include a view into your blog performance with metrics such as entrance and page views.
- **Campaign performance:** Evaluating the success of specific marketing campaigns against their objectives

and budgets. This is the performance metrics for the integrated campaigns that span digital, IR and events.
- **Qualitative soundbites**: Always capture and include a few short sentences or phrases from press, articles, social media, customers, etc. that spotlight positive takeaways. These sparkling gems help provide context and add a nice touch to an executive summary.

It's important to tailor the marketing scorecard to the specific needs and goals of the organization. Focus on a concise set of metrics that align with the business's strategic priorities and provide a holistic view of marketing performance. Additionally, using data visualization and trends analysis can enhance the scorecard's effectiveness in conveying information to executives.

A Scorecard for Optimization: This level of metrics is more specific in nature and provides the type of details that can help you drive program decisions on a day-to-day basis.

- **Marketing channel optimization**: Tracking the metrics and results of various marketing channels (e.g., social media, email, paid search) to identify which channels are most effective at driving traffic, leads, and conversions.
- **Website optimization:** Metrics such as page speed, server response time, etc. are vital to optimizing your website's performance.

A Scorecard for Cost-Effectiveness: Additionally, if your sales, marketing, and finance systems are integrated to enable more sophisticated tracking and calculations, return-on-investment (ROI), customer acquisition cost (CAC), and customer lifetime value (LTV) are three valuable metrics used to assess the cost-effectiveness and efficiency of marketing efforts. By including these metrics on a marketing scorecard, organizations gain a comprehensive understanding of the fiscal impact of their marketing initiatives.

- **ROI** measures the return generated from an investment relative to its cost, providing insight into the profitability of marketing campaigns. The ratio of the revenue generated from marketing campaigns to the cost of those campaigns. ROI provides a clear picture of the efficiency and effectiveness of marketing spend.
- **CAC** represents the cost incurred to acquire a new customer, encompassing expenses related to marketing and sales activities. The average cost to acquire a new customer. This metric helps evaluate the cost-effectiveness of acquiring new customers and can be compared to customer lifetime value (LTV).
- **LTV** is the average value of a customer over their entire relationship with the company. This metric demonstrates the long-term value of marketing efforts in retaining and upselling customers. Retaining existing customers is often more cost-effective than acquiring new ones, making this metric vital for long-term success.

And what about emerging trends? For many companies, it's voice of customer (VOC) analytics. VOC analytics is a strategic approach that involves capturing and analyzing customer feedback to improve marketing strategies by gaining insights into customer sentiments, preferences, and experiences. In the context of B2B marketing, understanding customer feedback is crucial for optimizing products, services, and overall customer satisfaction. There are various methods for capturing and analyzing customer feedback, and it's not expected that all of these are in play at all companies. But it is a list that can be leveraged. In addition to surveys and customer interviews, commonly used methods include:

- **Customer satisfaction (CSAT) and net promoter score (NPS)**: Metrics that gauge customer satisfaction and loyalty. These metrics provide insights into the customer experience and the likelihood of customers recommending the company to others. NPS is a widely used metric to gauge customer satisfaction and loyalty. B2B companies can use the Net Promoter Score by asking customers a simple question: "How likely are you to recommend our product/service to others?" Responses are categorized as promoters, passives, or detractors, providing a quick measure of overall satisfaction.

- **Social media listening**: Monitoring social media platforms for mentions, comments, and discussions related to the B2B brand provides real-time insights into customer sentiments. Social media listening tools can help track and analyze social mentions to understand public opinion and identify areas for improvement.

- **Customer feedback platforms**: Implementing customer feedback platforms allows B2B companies to collect and centralize feedback from various touchpoints. These platforms often include features such as sentiment analysis to understand the emotional tone of customer comments.

- **Customer advisory boards**: Establishing customer advisory boards involves inviting key customers to participate in strategic discussions. This forum allows customers to provide direct feedback, share insights, and collaborate with the company on future product development or enhancements.

- **Customer support and service interactions**: Analyzing interactions with customer support and service teams provides valuable insights into common issues, challenges, and areas that may need improvement. Customer support tickets and interactions can be analyzed for recurring themes.

- **Online reviews and testimonials**: B2B buyers often rely on reviews and testimonials when making

purchasing decisions. Monitoring and analyzing online reviews on platforms like Gartner Peer Insights, TrustRadius, or industry-specific review sites can offer insights into customer satisfaction and pain points.
- **Website feedback tools**: Implementing feedback tools on the company website allows visitors to provide input on their experience. These tools may include pop-up surveys, feedback forms, or chatbots that engage with visitors and gather feedback in real-time.

In B2B marketing, the integration of these methods helps create a holistic understanding of customer sentiments, preferences, and needs. Leveraging VOC analytics enables B2B companies to make data-driven decisions, enhance customer experiences, and continuously improve their products and services based on customer feedback.

> "Not everything that can be counted counts, and not everything that counts can be counted."
> - Albert Einstein

Think Indigo

Taking a break can lead to breakthroughs.

Here's a blank page to take a break
(and jot down some fresh thoughts and ideas).

Think Indigo

4

Be Passionate About …

In discussions about successful marketing planning, two often underestimated realms come into focus: **design and details**. Design stands as the hidden strength of influence behind every victorious marketing campaign, subtly shaping perceptions and capturing imaginations.

Simultaneously, attention to detail emerges as the hidden power propelling remarkable marketing executions. Many seasoned marketers acknowledge these dimensions as the most gratifying aspects of their craft—a realm where concepts and projects materialize with **visual flair and professional finesse**, marking the pinnacle of a job well executed.

If you can channel your passion towards recognizing the importance and value of both design and attention to detail and embrace the role of champion for these often-overlooked pillars, you will likely be rewarded. **They hold the potential to elevate marketing endeavors from good to extraordinary.**

> "There is no magic in magic. It's all in the details." – Walt Disney

Design

There are seven types of design in marketing that encompass various aspects of visual communication and user experience. Each type of design contributes uniquely to the overall marketing strategy, creating a cohesive and impactful visual identity across various channels. Effective design in marketing goes beyond aesthetics; it is a strategic tool that shapes perceptions, communicates messages, and enhances the overall experience for the audience. **Superior design encourages a viewer to want to see and learn more.** Here's a brief explanation of each:

- **Brand design** is the process of creating and shaping the visual elements that represent a brand. This includes the brand's logo, color palette, typography, and other visual assets. Brand design is of course crucial for establishing a brand's identity and conveying its personality. Consistent and compelling brand design helps build recognition, trust, and loyalty among consumers.
- **Graphic design** involves the creation of visual content for communication purposes. This includes designing marketing collateral such as brochures, posters, banners, and digital assets. Graphic design plays a significant role in conveying messages effectively. It combines text and images to create visually appealing and informative materials that capture the audience's attention and communicate key information.
- **Multi-media design** integrates various forms of media, including text, graphics, audio, video, and animations, to create engaging and interactive content. In a multimedia-driven landscape, this design type is pivotal for creating dynamic and immersive marketing experiences. It is used in presentations,

digital advertising, and interactive content that captivates and informs the audience.

- **Web design** involves the creation of visual elements and user interface for websites. It encompasses layout, navigation, color schemes, and overall aesthetics. Web design is critical for creating a positive user experience on websites. A well-designed website not only attracts visitors but also encourages engagement and conversions. It reflects the brand identity and enhances credibility.
- **User Interface (UI) design** focuses on optimizing the interaction between users and digital products. UI design deals with the visual aspects for digital products such as apps and websites. It ensures a user-friendly interface, smooth navigation, and a positive overall experience, contributing to customer satisfaction and loyalty.
- **Product design (whether UI or industrial design)** assumes a key role in the context of marketing as it profoundly shapes the perception of a product. A well-crafted product design is an incredibly strong marketing asset. It can draw in a larger customer base, elevate the user experience, and set the product apart from its competitors. Beyond aesthetics, it serves as a powerful communicator of the brand's value and identity. In essence, excellent product design transcends functionality; it becomes a compelling narrative that resonates with customers and reinforces the brand's position within the competitive landscape.
- **Environmental design** involves creating visual elements for physical spaces, such as office branding, signage, retail stores, exhibitions, or event spaces. It considers how people interact with the designed environment. Environmental design is vital for creating memorable brand experiences in physical spaces. It influences the atmosphere, layout, and

aesthetics of spaces where customers engage with a brand, impacting their perception and interaction.

The importance of design and creativity in marketing should never be underestimated. It plays a crucial role in modern marketing, contributing significantly to the success of businesses, including B2B companies.

Companies can make the mistake of not recognizing the skills required to have a talented design team – whether that team is in-house or via an agency.

Limiting designs to whatever resources they have, rather than getting the help of dedicated professionals can be a costly mistake. It can be observed in various aspects:

- **Brand recognition, visual appeal, and consistency:** Creative and well-designed visuals, logos, and branding materials enhance the visual appeal of a brand, making it memorable for the audience. Design ensures a consistent and cohesive brand identity across various marketing channels, creating a unified and recognizable brand image.
- **Storytelling and message clarity:** Creative elements help in telling a compelling brand or solution story. Effective storytelling through design can emotionally connect with the audience and communicate the brand's values and mission. Creativity in design helps in simplifying complex messages, making them more digestible and engaging for the audience.
- **User experience (UX) and engagement**: For B2B companies, a well-designed website and user interfaces contribute to a positive user experience. An intuitive and visually appealing design encourages engagement and interaction. Creativity in content formats, such as interactive infographics, quizzes, and

videos, enhances user engagement and encourages participation.
- **Differentiation in a crowded market**: In a competitive market, creative and distinctive design helps a B2B company stand out from the crowd. It contributes to the development of a unique visual identity that sets the brand apart from competitors. Creativity allows for the development of visual differentiators that can become signature elements associated with the brand.
- **Shareability and social media**: Visual elements are crucial for content marketing success. Eye-catching graphics, images, and videos are more likely to capture the audience's attention on social media and other content-sharing platforms. Creative and visually appealing content is more likely to be shared, expanding the reach of the brand's message and content.
- **Emotional connection and ad campaign effectiveness:** Advertising agencies bring creative expertise to develop impactful ad campaigns. Creativity in ad design can enhance message recall and increase the effectiveness of advertising efforts. Well-designed advertisements have the power to evoke emotions and create a lasting impression on the audience.

The value that an advertising agency brings to a B2B company lies in its ability to infuse creativity and design excellence **into every aspect of marketing**. From branding to advertising, website design to content creation, a creative and well-executed approach enhances the overall effectiveness of marketing efforts and contributes to building a strong and memorable brand presence.

> "There are three responses to a piece of design – yes, no and WOW! Wow is the one to aim for." – Milton Glaser

It's also important to leverage your design resources as an educator. They can help your marketing, product, and sales teams with the application of basic **design principles** that are instrumental in creating visually appealing and effective communications. For example, the first is balance and proportion. The second is contrast and emphasis. And the third is movement and unity. Together, they serve as good guiding principles for marketers to craft more visually engaging and impactful materials.

- **Balance and proportion**: Balance is the distribution of visual elements within a design to create equilibrium. It ensures that no single element overpowers the others, promoting a harmonious and visually stable composition. In marketing, achieving balance helps convey a sense of order and professionalism in visual materials. Proportion refers to the size and scale of elements in relation to one another. Maintaining proper proportion in marketing design ensures that visual elements are appropriately sized, creating a balanced and aesthetically pleasing composition. It helps avoid visual distortions and communicates a sense of harmony.
- **Contrast and emphasis**: Contrast involves the juxtaposition of different elements to create visual interest and highlight key components. In marketing, contrast is used to draw attention to specific messages or elements, making them stand out. It enhances readability and ensures essential information is easily noticed. Emphasis, also known as dominance, refers to the prioritization of certain elements to create focal points. In marketing, establishing dominance helps guide the viewer's attention to the most crucial

aspects of the message or design, reinforcing key brand or product attributes. It is typically achieved using size, font choice or color combinations.
- **Movement and visual unity**: Movement, sometimes also referred to as hierarchy, involves organizing elements in a way that signifies their importance. In marketing design, hierarchy ensures that information is presented in a logical order, moving to guide the viewer's eyes from the most critical details to supporting information. It aids in conveying a clear and organized message. Unity brings together various elements in a design to create a cohesive and harmonious whole. In marketing, unity ensures that all visual elements work together seamlessly, reinforcing the brand identity and delivering a consistent message. A unified design has harmony, enhances brand recognition, and strengthens the overall impact.

Incorporating these design principles into marketing materials enhances the visual appeal, clarity, and effectiveness of communication. Whether in print, digital media, or other marketing collateral, a thoughtful application of these principles helps marketers create visually compelling and memorable content that resonates with their target audience. At a minimum, be a design advocate and have your own list of tips to share.

- Keep things simple.
- Check placements and alignment.
- Utilize white space and allow **breathing room**. White space refers to the blank areas of a piece. It can help organize the elements and emphasize the most important ones and helps to create an aura of clarity, luxury, and minimalism. Too little white space can create a cluttered and over-crowded appearance.
- Add an element of contrast such as a **pop of color**.

- Stay consistent and in support of your brand; always apply the style guide.

Details

In the realm of marketing, attention to detail is not just a commendable trait—it's a critical component of successful execution. The smallest elements can make or break a campaign, influencing how your audience perceives your brand, product, and its professionalism. Details matter in every aspect, from the accuracy of your messaging to the visual appeal of your content and the seamless functionality of your digital platforms.

A meticulously planned strategy can fall flat if executed poorly. Even some minor mistakes can send a message to customers that your brand lacks the reliability and quality they seek.

Consider a few common yet detrimental errors:

- **Typos and grammatical errors**: These can occur in social media posts, email newsletters, or website content. For example, a well-known tech company once sent out an email with a glaring typo in the subject line, resulting in a wave of online ridicule and a hit to their credibility.
- **Broken links**: In digital marketing, broken links can frustrate potential customers. Imagine a retail company promoting a sale via email, but the link to the sale page is broken. Not only does this frustrate users, but it also results in lost sales opportunities.
- **Inconsistent branding**: Visual and tonal inconsistencies across different platforms can confuse and alienate your audience. For example, a company's

website might have a sleek, modern design, but their social media graphics are outdated and amateurish.

Having a team member who's passionate about the finer points can make all the difference - someone who encourages others to pause and consider the impact of even the smallest details before rushing ahead.

Whenever this topic comes up, I think of my long-time friend and close marketing colleague, Mary Jane Viscomi. Among numerous talents, **she has this remarkable ability to balance the pursuit of perfection with the practicality of getting things done.**

MJ recently brought up an interesting point that stayed with me. She attributed her technical mindset - likely shaped by her engineering background - to her keen eye for detail. Perhaps a hidden superpower to those of us in technical marketing. "Maybe it's the engineer in me," she said, "but details matter. Not just in the content we create, but in solving the operational problems that come up along the way."

She went on to illustrate this with a recent example. The sales development representative (SDR) team had noticed they weren't receiving certain customer inquiries from a partner summit. They quickly blamed the website chatbot tool and left it at that. But MJ, true to form, decided to dig deeper. She discovered that the real issue wasn't with the chatbot at all; it was a simple human error—a partner hadn't set the correct flag indicating they were away. Because of her attention to detail, the system was updated to automatically detect when partners are unavailable, preventing future issues. It took a bit of time, some due diligence, and a touch of persistence—but as MJ always says, nine times out of ten, it's well worth the effort.

To help ensure that you don't overlook the important details, consider the following strategies:

Develop a detailed checklist: Before launching any campaign, have a comprehensive checklist that covers all aspects, from proofreading content to testing links and ensuring brand consistency.

Utilize quality assurance processes: Implement thorough QA processes for all marketing materials. This could involve multiple team members reviewing and testing content across different devices and platforms.

Encourage a detail-oriented culture: Foster a workplace culture that values attention to detail. Provide training and resources to help your team develop a keen eye for detail and an understanding of its importance.

Use technology to assist: Leverage tools like Grammarly for proofreading, link checkers for verifying URLs, and project management software to track tasks and ensure nothing is overlooked.

By placing a high priority on details, marketing teams can enhance their execution, ensuring that every campaign not only reaches but also resonates with its intended audience. In a competitive landscape, meticulous attention to detail can be the difference between a successful campaign and a costly blunder.

> "The difference between something good and something great is attention to detail.' – Charles R. Swindoll, pastor and author

5

Go-to-Market with Confidence

In today's fast-paced landscape, innovation stands as the livelihood that propels companies forward, promoting growth and resilience. Innovation is not merely a buzzword; it's the heartbeat of progress. And as we navigate the ever-evolving demands of industries and markets, the thrill of bringing new solutions to market is unparalleled. The energy emanating from a company poised to launch groundbreaking new products is unmistakable—it's the culmination of tireless research, creative ideation, and unwavering dedication.

In other words, the importance of new B2B product launches cannot be overstated. In a world where change is the only constant, businesses must adapt and lead. These launches are not just about unveiling features; they signify our commitment to pushing boundaries, challenging the status quo, and delivering unparalleled value to our partners and customers.

Model a Launch Strategy

For marketers, it's crucial to first grasp the difference between a Go-To-Market (GTM) strategy and a product launch. They are related concepts within the broader space of business and marketing, but they serve distinct purposes and involve distinct aspects of a company's overall strategy. Ensuring clarity on this distinction within your organization can contribute to a broader understanding of the roles played by product management, product marketing, and marketing—a challenge that many companies wrestle with when it comes to clear definition and organization.

- The GTM strategy serves as the overarching framework that guides how a company will bring all its products to market. It provides strategic direction and alignment with overall business objectives.
- A product launch is one of the tactical elements within the GTM strategy, executed to introduce a specific product to the market in a compelling and effective manner.
- While the GTM strategy is more enduring and encompasses the entire business, a product launch is a temporary and targeted effort designed to make a significant impact during a specific period.

In essence, a GTM strategy is the master plan that guides how a company will navigate the market, while a product launch is the carefully orchestrated moment when a new product takes center stage in the market's spotlight.

Go-To-Market | Pragmatic marketing framework

STRATEGY						EXECUTION		
			Business plan	Positioning	Marketing plan			
Market problems	Market definition	Pricing	Buyer experience	Revenue growth				
Win/Loss analysis	Distribution strategy	Buy, build or partner	Buyer personas	Revenue retention				
Distinctive competency	Product portfolio	Product profitability	User personas	**Launch**				
Market	Focus	Business	Planning	Programs	Enablement	Support		
Competitive landscape	Product roadmap	Innovation	RQMTs	Awareness	Sales alignment	Programs		
Asset assessment			Use scenarios	Nurturing	Content	Operations		
			Stakeholder comms	Advocacy	Sales tools	Events		
				Metrics	Channel training	Channels		

Source: Pragmatic Institute

The GTM strategy is broader and more holistic, addressing not only the launch of a specific product but the overall approach to entering and succeeding in the market, typically driven by the executive leadership suite and product management.

Both are crucial components of a company's overall business strategy, working together to achieve success in a competitive and dynamic business environment. This book is not about the many facets of a company's GTM process and strategy. That is a complete topic on its own. Instead, many of the marketing-oriented components of a broader GTM strategy have already been touched upon – audience, positioning, messaging, marketing plan, promotion, etc. This section will focus on modeling an approach to product launch planning.

One of the most important things a business will do is the launch of a new product(s).

In product management, the distinctions between minor releases, major releases, and new product launches are significant and pertain to the scale and impact of the changes being introduced.

Effective product management involves a balanced approach, incorporating these distinct types of launches based on the product roadmap, market needs, and overall business strategy.

It's vital that marketing has an advanced view, across the organization, of all new initiatives coming to market. **It is not uncommon for marketing to be approached ad hoc by individual teams, randomly prior to a release, looking for various levels of support.**

Like gate processes on the product and development side, marketing teams should be proactive in mapping out the calendar and getting agreement as to the **categorization and appropriate type of support** – including budget and resources. One straightforward approach is to leverage three categories: minor release, major release, and new product launch.

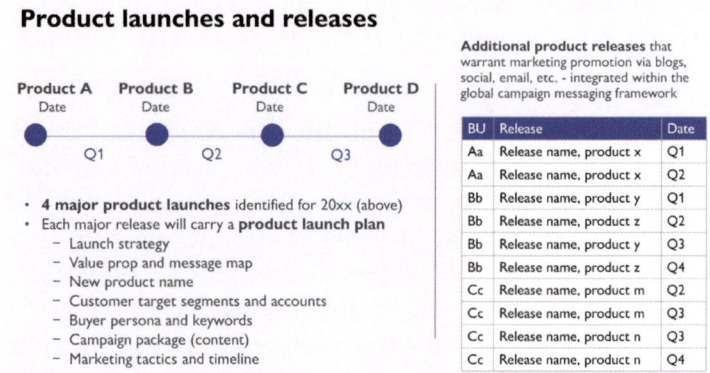

Minor and Major Releases

If it is **a release on an existing product,** is the release considered a major or minor release? A product management team should provide a clear designation for marketing so they can more easily determine the appropriate level of marketing support. Commonly, minor and major releases are defined as follows.

Minor releases involve small-scale changes, often addressing software bug fixes, minor enhancements, or optimizations. They are typically more frequent and occur in response to ongoing maintenance needs or the identification of minor issues. The impact on users is minimal, and these releases are often transparent to end-users. They are intended to improve the product's stability and address specific issues and typically have a small revenue impact. The release process for minor updates is usually streamlined and quicker compared to major releases.

Major releases encompass significant changes to the product, including the introduction of new features, functionalities, or innovations. They are less frequent compared to minor releases and are often planned as part of a strategic roadmap, aligning with the overall product vision. Major releases have a more noticeable impact on users, as they introduce substantial improvements or new capabilities. Communication with users is crucial during major releases to inform them about the upcoming changes, provide training if necessary, and manage expectations. Major releases may have a more significant revenue impact, are newsworthy to the market, may be positioning the company as innovative, regionally significant or in a new market segment.

New Products and Solutions

If it is a **new product or solution**, is the team ready for marketing engagement?

Introducing entirely new products or solutions involves the creation of something that didn't exist in the product portfolio before. This can include expansions into new markets, new product lines, or entirely innovative offerings. Launching entirely new products is infrequent and usually aligned with strategic business goals or market opportunities. The impact is substantial, potentially reshaping the company's position in the market or addressing entirely new customer needs. It often requires a significant investment of resources. Launching new products involves a comprehensive go-to-market strategy, including market research, positioning, pricing, and extensive marketing efforts.

> In a recent conversation with Jessica Beadman, a favorite coworker of mine, and one of the most knowledgeable (and enjoyable!) marketing professionals I know ...

… I asked her if she could provide her perspective on the topic, if she had any advice to share.

Jessica is a seasoned marketing leader, mentor, and coach – located just across the pond in Paignton, England. Her expertise spans a broad spectrum, encompassing global marketing communications, public relations, events management, digital marketing, social media management, and campaign planning and execution.

She believes when new initiatives first emerge, it's crucial to gain alignment upfront, gathering vital information, with due diligence and documentation. Too often, marketing teams are tasked with launching a new product without essential details for building a solid plan. Jessica underscores the importance of **asking the right questions** and collaborating closely with the product team to ensure clarity and understanding.

To facilitate this, she put together what she calls a "**GTM Readiness Kit**" for new product launches – four steps to provide marketing with the necessary information they need to help the business succeed. Jessica explains that the goal of the kit is to address misalignment between sales, marketing, and product management *before* going to market with a new product.

Additionally, the kit acts as a "**marketing shield**", protecting the marketing team from unwarranted blame when a product's success doesn't materialize as planned. She notes that marketing can often find itself in a crossfire, with product launch plans inaccurately blamed for a product's misstep or even failure.

To counteract this, it's crucial to document what is known - and unknown - well before building the plan. This approach helps clarify what information was available when product management engaged with marketing, and equally important, what information was missing. For organizations where marketing and sales are not included early in the product gate process, Jessica's approach offers a means to help marketing teams insert themselves.

Step One: Summarize business alignment, vision, and goals.

Product marketing teams can utilize the following list of questions as a required first step for product owners to engage with marketing. It's critical information, and product owners should be more than willing to provide detailed answers for each. If they are reluctant or claim to be too busy, consider it a significant red flag.

- What's the current market opportunity?
- How does the product align with the company's strategy?
- How does the product fit within existing product lines?
- What are your goals for revenue growth?
- How will success be measured? What are the expectations within the first 100 days post-launch in terms of engaged prospects or opportunities?
- What additional services and support are associated with the product?
- Have the distribution channels been determined? Will it be sold through direct sales, channel partners, strategic partners, etc.?
- Is sales leadership onboard with the go-to-market goals?
- Are there any regional particulars?
- Is this business development or sales ready?
- What is the timing for launch? Are there any specific events or drivers influencing the launch date?
- What are the proof points? Is the problem that the product addresses widely recognized, or does it require further validation?

- Are there defined use cases and measurable benefits?
- Who are the main competitors and what makes the product unique?

Step Two: Layout the timeline.

As a second step in the kit, product marketing can use the following template to start visualizing the product launch plan from a timeline perspective. This involves collaborating closely with product owners and sales to gather essential (and honest) schedule information.

- What are the dates for gate reviews and key milestones, including the expected sales readiness and launch-to-market date?
- Are there any significant risks that have been identified which could potentially impact the launch timing?

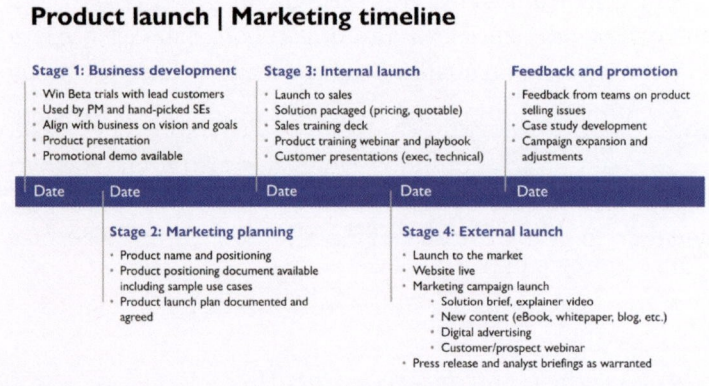

When laying out the timeline, it's beneficial to divide it into four stages: business development, marketing preparation, internal launch, and external launch. This approach helps present a more comprehensive (and realistic) view.

Remember, fluidity and flexibility are key in a successful product launch. The external marketing campaign of a new product often begins several months before the official release date, typically not exceeding three months. However, product release dates can sometimes shift unexpectedly. Rather than concentrating all efforts on a single launch date, it's beneficial to spread the campaign across several weeks and phases. This phased approach not only helps generate a sustained buildup of interest and engagement leading up to the launch but also allows you to maintain and expand the narrative beyond the initial release, capitalizing on the ongoing excitement.

Step Three: Align on the foundation.

Step three involves aligning on the foundation of your marketing strategy. As emphasized in Chapter 3, it's crucial to get grounded in the basics, get set with the fundamentals. This means working closely with sales to understand the potential customer, working closely with the product team to understand the intended value proposition, and working closely with corporate marketing to shape the right positioning and message. The key elements to align on are:

- ✓ **Audience.** Define the target audience, including use cases and scenarios of how they will interact with your product.
- ✓ **Value.** Establish your value proposition, highlighting what sets your product apart in the market and why it is beneficial to the customer.
- ✓ **Voice.** Determine the product's voice and key messages, including proof points that support your claims and build credibility.

Step Four: Craft a creative launch campaign.

Once you have the information you need and have aligned on the foundation, the next step is to **follow the established process for building out the tactics of your integrated marketing campaign, as discussed in Chapter 4**. In this case, your "story" revolves around the new product launch.

Additionally, **now is the perfect time to unleash your creativity**. The online world is a treasure trove of innovative ideas and examples to spark your imagination. For example, consider incorporating pre-launch teasers or sneak peeks to generate anticipation and curiosity, leveraging short and sweet demo videos on social media. Consider collaborating with an influencer and holding a launch event, including early access offers or an element of exclusivity.

And lastly, **be prepared to communicate your plan effectively**. Product launches often draw significant attention, so be ready to present and share - sometimes frequently and to various levels - within an organization. Start with a high-level overview and then delve into the details as needed. The following is one example of an initial format to highlight major deliverables.

Regardless of your company size or industry, there's nothing more energizing than the launch of an exciting new product. And while a great name won't make a mediocre product better, a great name can be a big part of your launch success.

The Name Game

Product naming plays a pivotal role in shaping a brand's identity, influencing perceptions, and driving market success. A well-chosen name not only captures the essence of the product but also resonates with the target audience, fostering connection and recognition. But to be frank, naming technology products can be a very painful exercise. If you've been through the process, you're likely all too familiar with some of the frustrating scenarios.

- The lead developer and their team came up with "the perfect" name that they love. Although it doesn't align with the brand, nor fit with the business - they don't understand why it's important to remain objective and explore options.
- The product names across the company portfolio look like an ill-assorted collection of mismatched socks. Although there may be some resemblance of an attempt to coordinate, too many times the name was left up to whomever was leading the project to select.
- A talented agency presents a strong selection of candidates to the team – well-thought out and well-aligned, with the right amount of creativity to peak interest and intrigue. They are met with random personal reasons as to what they don't like about each one. They say things like this one is 'not technical enough' or that one sounds like a word my sister always used.

There's a great deal of research and advice available online that can guide you on how to name products, but for purposes here, it's important to stay grounded in a few key aspects.

First, start with your current brand architecture. Map out the product names of your current portfolio. It may appear rather ugly, or it may be impressive. Either way, it's vital to create it, share it openly with various teams, ask for their input if you are missing anything. Awareness and completeness are the objectives.

This will ensure that everyone staked in the new product name process has a broader vision of the context – the portfolio and how things do or do not fit together. It will help you explain that names must be both a good fit for the individual product, but also a working part of the more cohesive brand name architecture for the whole company.

Second, have product naming guidelines. Ideally, you can incorporate them into your company's brand guidelines and documentation if they have such. Having a naming strategy and rules will be a valuable framework for making the process easier going forward.

Your guidelines may begin with something as simple as:

- **Be reflective of the brand**: The product name should align with the brand's values, mission, and overall identity. It should evoke the desired emotions and associations that the brand seeks to convey.
- **Be clear and memorable**: A good product name is easy to pronounce, spell, and remember. It should be concise yet descriptive, instantly conveying the product's purpose or key benefit.
- **Be unique and distinctive**: To stand out in a crowded marketplace, the product name should be distinct from competitors and avoid any potential confusion with existing brands or trademarks. A compelling product name can tell a story, evoke emotions, or convey a unique selling proposition. Consider incorporating storytelling elements or innovative language to differentiate the product and pique curiosity. Before finalizing a product name, conduct thorough trademark research to ensure its

availability and legal protection. Avoid names that are already trademarked or could lead to potential infringement issues.
- **Be relevant to your audience**: Consider the preferences, interests, and language of the target audience when selecting a product name. It should resonate with their needs, aspirations, and values to establish a meaningful connection. If the product has potential for international expansion, ensure that the name is culturally sensitive, universally understood, and does not carry negative connotations in other languages or regions.
- **Be future proof**: Anticipate future trends, market shifts, and potential product expansions when selecting a name. Choose a name that can withstand the test of time and remain relevant as the brand evolves.

In terms of preferred approaches, there are various naming strategies to consider, including descriptive names (which directly describe the product's function or features), evocative names (which evoke certain emotions or imagery), coined names (which are invented or created), and symbolic names (which convey abstract concepts or values). Each approach has its own advantages and considerations, depending on the brand's positioning, target audience, and marketing objectives. **Your guidelines can outline when you would leverage more descriptive names, or extensions of existing product names, vs. when you would embark on a more abstract naming exercise.** Many times, the latter is reserved for major product launches, as the name itself must also be introduced and explained to the market requiring additional resources.

Ultimately, a successful product name is simply one that effectively communicates, resonates with customers, and supports the brand's essence. Keeping a few things in mind (the following list of favorite Don'ts) will help make the exercise and result much more rewarding.

> Don't ever ask the teams if they like it.
> Ask them, "Is it right?"

- **Don't rush the process**: Naming a product is a critical decision that requires careful consideration and research. Avoid rushing the process or settling for the first name that comes to mind.
- **Don't limit creativity**: While simplicity is important, don't shy away from creativity and innovation in naming. Explore different approaches and brainstorming techniques to generate unique and memorable name ideas.
- **Don't ignore feedback**: Once you've narrowed down potential names, gather feedback from stakeholders, focus groups, or target customers. Take feedback seriously and be open to constructive criticism, while also aware of personal opinions. Ignoring feedback can lead to missed opportunities or unintended consequences. If viable, conducting tests and iterations can help refine the name and ensure its effectiveness in resonating with the intended audience.
- **Don't overcomplicate:** Avoid overly complex or abstract names that may confuse or alienate potential customers. Keep the name straightforward and focused on communicating the product's value proposition.
- **Don't forget about SEO**: Consider the searchability and online visibility of the product name. How will your new product name perform in the search engines? How expensive would it be to advertise using that word? Decide on a name that is SEO-

friendly and aligns with relevant keywords or search terms to improve online discoverability.
- **Don't neglect legal considerations:** Ensure that the chosen name is legally available for use and does not infringe on trademarks or intellectual property rights. Failure to do so can result in costly legal disputes and brand reputation damage.
- **Don't settle for mediocrity:** Aim for a name that stands out and captures attention in the marketplace. Avoid generic or uninspired names that blend into the background and fail to differentiate the product from competitors.

Sell the Sellers

I have always believed that before you can sell anything to your customers, you must first sell it to the sellers. The sales organization should be excited about the product, understand the product and its value, and have confidence in their knowledge and available resources.

So, first and foremost, it must be about the team. Sales and marketing. Marketing and sales. That's why it's so critically important for both to work together in a collaborative and aligned manner. When both teams are working towards a common goal and have a shared understanding of the target audience, the brand messaging, and the customer journey, it can lead to increased revenue, higher customer satisfaction, and a stronger overall brand.

Yet sales and marketing misalignment is a common issue in many organizations, particularly in those where the two functions operate independently and do not have regular communication or collaboration. The conflict between sales and marketing teams often stems from a lack of alignment. Marketing teams are responsible for creating awareness, generating leads, and building relationships with potential customers, while sales teams are responsible for converting those leads into paying customers. When there is a disconnect, it can lead to tension, frustration, and missed opportunities.

For example, marketing teams may feel that their efforts are not being effectively leveraged by the sales team, while sales teams may feel that the leads generated by marketing are not of high quality or are not being followed up on in a timely manner.

However, with the right approach, it's possible to align these two functions and drive greater success for the organization. Some of the strategies that can help improve sales and marketing alignment include regular communication and collaboration, shared goals and metrics, a unified approach to customer data, and a focus on the customer journey. At the heart of the sales and marketing relationship sits content.

At the heart of the sales and marketing relationship sits content

Campaign content | Presentations and slides | Product playbooks | Weekly newsletter

In my experience, the range of potential sales enablement materials can be quite extensive. Therefore, it's beneficial to focus first on mastering the fundamentals. These four primary resources (campaign content, presentations, product playbooks, and newsletters), when done well, are likely to be well received.

#1. Package up your marketing campaign content.

This is a collection of content that is designed to be shared directly with prospects. This is all your marketing content (blogs, social posts, eBooks, case studies, etc.) that is available for your campaigns, that we covered previously in Chapter 3. **It should always do double duty**. Work for the campaigns, and work as a sales resource, allowing sales reps to touch prospects directly at periodic intervals with engaging information. **However, having all this great content available to sales is only half the battle.**

- You must first organize it well, so that sales reps **know when and how to use the content** and can easily locate it. For example, there is content you created that was geared to open doors (educational), to go into details of the solution (solution) and to get technical (selection stage). It should not just be a list, but a curated interface that guides them through the story to tell.
- Secondly, you must also provide them with accompanying **social posts and email templates** so they can easily send the content out. We all know how tricky it can be to write perfect posts and succinct, compelling emails. Don't leave this task to your sales team to try and figure it out on their own.

#2. Build a library of interchangeable short presentations.

Curate a centralized repository of slides that sales associates can easily access to tailor their presentations to specific customer needs and preferences, ensuring relevance and engagement. Break down presentations into modular components or building blocks that can be easily rearranged, combined, or omitted as needed. This modular approach allows sales associates to customize presentations more easily on the fly, adapting them to different audiences and situations.

#3. Create a foundational Product Playbook.

Don't overlook the need for capturing and communicating the basics of each of your products in a simple and straightforward language that everyone can understand. Well-written and well-designed playbooks will serve as a truly invaluable resource. Some common components include:

- **A product spotlight** that contains a product overview, your elevator pitch and value props, plus key product highlights (the most important things for sales to showcase).
- **Example dialogue.** This is pre-scripted messaging and talking points, in the form of leading customer questions and sample sales response. This content helps reps better prepare for an initial sales conversation.
- **Qualifying questions.** Geared towards Sales Development Representatives (SDRs), these are particularly helpful if you've got a team who is not overly experienced in a broad portfolio. These are broken into three areas:
    o **Discovery questions** for the salesperson to get a feel of the prospect's current challenges, their goals, and whether they've used a similar solution before.
    o **Product specific questions** that allow the salesperson to go deeper in understanding what gaps the prospect may have.
    o **General questions** for the salesperson to gauge decision making process, budget, timeline, and other product considerations from competitors.

- **Featured resources.** Collect the most relevant content to provide a list of key resources (including where to locate them).
- **A glossary of terms.** Don't assume that everyone knows all the acronyms. A glossary is always helpful with B2B technology.
- **Related products.** In some larger organizations, you may have opportunities to look outside of your own portfolio and expand a client's understanding of the company's broader product suite. It's a smart approach to recommend for sales, any related products to aid them in that conversation.

#4. Publish an internal newsletter, a Product Insider.

Delivered monthly via email from the product marketing team to your sales organization, this type of newsletter is a terrific means to continually communicate the latest product news, resources, and insights in a consolidated and consistent manner. It allows you to keep your teams informed about updates on product releases and promotions, recent press coverage, highlights of key wins, upcoming events, and newly available content—all curated from a marketing perspective to empower sales.

Stay connected with your field marketing team.

Working tightly with your field marketing team is essential. Not only does it promote success in specific geographic regions or markets, but they are your partner in key aspects of sales enablement. So, how does product marketing typically collaborate with the field? Although they of course collaborate on the planning, execution, and measurement of marketing campaigns and initiatives, there are three primary areas of importance.

- **Customization for local markets**: Field marketing teams have a deep understanding of local market

dynamics, customer preferences, and competitive landscapes. They collaborate with product marketing teams to customize messaging, content, and campaigns to resonate with target audiences in their respective regions.
- **Event planning and execution**: Field marketing teams often organize and host events such as trade shows, conferences, seminars, and workshops in their regions. Product marketing teams support these efforts by providing event-specific messaging, content, and promotional materials to drive engagement and generate leads.
- **Feedback loop**: Field marketing teams serve as the frontline representatives of the company in their regions and interact directly with customers, partners, and prospects. They provide valuable feedback to product marketing teams on market trends, customer needs, competitive insights, and the effectiveness of marketing programs.

How do you figure out what content your sales team really needs? Ask them.

Through close collaboration, product marketing and field marketing teams can ensure that marketing and sales enablement efforts are harmonized, localized, and optimized for maximum impact and success. Together, these teams remain closely connected to sales activities and data, monitoring content consumption metrics such as views, downloads, and sends. While responses may vary depending on organizational variables, it's crucial to maintain an open line of communication, attentively listening and responding to sales needs.

However, it's important to exercise caution when acting upon requests for new or varied content, as saying yes to everything can lead to overwhelming complexity and unnecessary clutter.

Striking a balance between responsiveness and selectivity is key to avoiding content overload and ensuring that resources are invested wisely for long-term effectiveness.

Think Indigo

6

Look Up

As the previous chapters laid the groundwork for crafting a sound plan, the next pivotal step is to elevate your perspective. Imagine "looking up" to see the entire landscape rather than just the immediate path ahead. This broader context will be essential as you refine and execute your strategy.

The advice to "look up" carries some useful wisdom in a world where our attention is often absorbed by the specifics of daily tasks, smartphones, and immediate concerns. In the hustle of it all, it's easy to become immersed in the downward details — staring down at screens, fixating on immediate challenges, and navigating the intricacies of our work.

However, true magic often happens when we consciously choose to look up. This isn't just a physical act of redirecting our gaze; **it's a powerful metaphor for shifting our mindset**. It's an invitation to elevate our perspective, broaden our horizons, and embrace the bigger picture. So, what does it do?

- **It helps you illustrate a leadership perspective.** Encouraging the team around you to look up fosters a trait of visionary leadership. It allows you to align with the organization's overarching goals and values and invites others to do the same.
- **It allows you to break from the routine.** Routine can be a comfort, but it can also be limiting, especially

in the world of product and marketing. Looking up prompts us to break from the familiar and explore new possibilities. It's an antidote to stagnation and a catalyst for innovation.

- **It can move you to seek inspiration.** Looking up is an invitation to seek inspiration from new places - nature, art, conversations, or mentors. Inspiration often resides in the spaces beyond our immediate surroundings.
- **It assists you in cultivating empathy.** Looking up also symbolizes a conscious effort to see things from someone else's point of view, understand their perspectives, and cultivate empathy. Empathy helps you connect with both colleagues and customers in a much more authentic way.
- **It lets you see the bigger picture.** We all navigate an endless series of experiences, opportunities, and connections. When we look up, we gain a panoramic view of the bigger picture. It's a reminder that our current challenges are just a small part of a larger narrative. By embracing this broader perspective, we can make more informed decisions, understand the interconnectedness of our actions, and navigate our journey with purpose.
- **It encourages growth.** Personal and professional growth often requires us to lift our sights beyond the immediate horizon. Whether it's expanding our knowledge, taking on new challenges, or pursuing ambitious goals, the act of looking up signifies a commitment to continuous growth. It's an acknowledgment that there is always more to learn, achieve, and aspire to.

In essence, looking up is a rallying call to transcend the ordinary, embrace the extraordinary, and chart a more expansive course. It's a reminder that the sky above is limitless, and so are the possibilities when we choose to lift our heads.

> **As you look up, picture yourself constructing a building where each story represents a new and elevated level of achievement.**

The term "stories" to refer to the levels of buildings has an interesting historical origin. The usage can be traced back to medieval Europe when architects and builders incorporated narrative elements into the design of structures.

In the Gothic period, which spanned from the 12th to the 16th century, builders constructed magnificent cathedrals with towering spires and intricate designs. These structures often featured sculptures, carvings, and stained-glass windows that depicted biblical stories and religious narratives. As one looked up from the ground floor, **it was akin to reading a visual storybook**, with each level of the cathedral telling a different part of the narrative.

The concept of dividing buildings into distinct levels, each with its own purpose and design, persisted over time. By the 19th century, when skyscrapers began to emerge in urban landscapes, the term "stories" became a practical way to describe the various levels or floors of these tall buildings.

So, when we refer to the levels of a building as "stories" today, we are, in a way, continuing a tradition that draws on the idea of a building as a visual and architectural narrative, where each floor represents a new chapter or level in the overall story of the structure.

The stories that follow represent the different levels of my journey, each one helping me to look up and encouraging my team to do the same. What are your stories? Take the time to reflect on your own experiences and define the areas you want to take on.

Help Others Find Their Marketing Voice

Here on the first floor, it's all about amplification: how you can and should mobilize others to broaden your reach.

In the modern marketing landscape, the voice of a company is now significantly shaped by its employees and their interactions with the marketplace. Employees are the most credible and authentic spokespeople for your product and brand, bringing a human element to marketing that traditional advertising often lacks. By sharing their genuine experiences and insights, employees can create a more relatable and trustworthy image – becoming an extremely powerful resource in your marketing mix. Helping your co-workers and the company's employees find their marketing voice doesn't happen overnight but can be quite rewarding when you succeed (both personally and professionally). There are three principal areas to focus on.

- **Social media advocacy**: Employees sharing company news, products, or their work experiences on social media platforms can greatly enhance visibility. According to the Edelman Trust Barometer, employees are trusted more than CEOs and corporate communications.[4] Authentic content from employees is more likely to be trusted by the audience, thereby enhancing credibility. In addition, each employee likely has their own network, which can be leveraged to amplify your messaging, significantly extending the reach of your communications. Some employees

---

[4] '2023 Edelman Trust Barometer Reveals Business is the Only Institution Viewed as Ethical and Competent', Edelman, accessed June 2, 2024, https://www.edelman.com/news-awards/2023-edelman-trust-barometer.

though, may not be comfortable with how, when and what to post. You can help them.
- **Content creation**: Encouraging employees to work with you to write blog posts, participate in webinars, or create videos about their expertise and experiences can help diversify positioning the company as a thought leader in its industry. However, some employees with valuable information and stories to share are simply not strong writers nor creators. You can help them.
- **Thought leadership**: Employees interacting with customers through community forums and public events can amplify messages and create lasting positive impressions. Yet some people may need encouragement, confidence, or media training to discover their hidden talent for confident public speaking. You can help them.

Leveraging the voices of employees for amplification is crucial in today's marketing environment. It adds authenticity, extends reach, and engages both employees and the audience. Marketing teams must foster a culture where employees feel empowered and equipped to share the company's messages effectively. This approach not only enhances brand and product visibility but also builds a stronger, more connected workforce.

It's important to note however, this is not simply a matter of "here's the articles we want you to post and share." It's identifying the employees that are interested – then working with them to build their marketing knowledge, level of comfort, and engagement. The conversation is about personal branding, what's in for the company, but also what's in it for them.

Leveraging the voices of employees for brand and product amplification offers significant benefits not only to the company but also to the employees themselves. For employees, actively participating in advocacy can help build their own personal brand, establishing their identity and credibility within their industry. By sharing their expertise and insights, employees can position themselves as thought leaders and industry influencers. This visibility can lead to professional growth opportunities, such as speaking engagements, networking prospects, and career advancement.

Additionally, employees who actively contribute to amplification can gain recognition within their organization, enhancing their reputation among peers and leadership. This involvement demonstrates initiative, expertise, and a commitment to the company's success, which can be beneficial during performance reviews and promotions.

A highly acclaimed book on personal branding that serves as an excellent resource is *Known* by Mark W. Schaefer. Scheafer, a bestselling author of some of the world's most beloved marketing books, explains that "becoming known is about approaching your digital life with an intent that establishes the authority, reputation, and audience to achieve your goals." [5] This insightful book makes a great gift from a marketing team to those interested in positioning themselves publicly in your industry.

How you approach helping others to find their marketing voice may vary depending on time and resources of course. But there's a few areas to consider when pulling together your plan of action.

- **Training and resources**: Provide employees with training and resources on how to effectively communicate your product's message. This can include social media guidelines, key messaging points, and content creation tips.

---

[5] Mark W. Schaefer, *Known*, (Publisher Mark W. Schaefer, 2017), p. back cover.

- **Incentives and recognition**: Recognize and reward employees who actively participate in your product's amplification. This can be through formal recognition programs, bonuses, or public acknowledgments.
- **Content collaboration**: Involve employees in content creation processes. For example, collaborate with them to write blog posts, create videos, or develop case studies **that highlight their work** and insights.
- **Communication channels**: Establish clear and open communication channels where employees can share their content ideas and receive feedback. This encourages a culture of continuous improvement and active participation.

In summary, employee advocacy not only amplifies the company's message but also empowers employees to grow their professional presence, fostering a mutually beneficial relationship.

Learn to Pivot

On the second floor, the focus is on agility.

Learning to pivot can mean a lot of different things. But to me, this floor was about being agile, not being afraid to move on, and a willingness to try new things.

Be agile. Executing a marketing plan can be wrought with tons of moving parts and pieces, in addition to changing priorities and unexpected interruptions and adjustments. It's imperative to be agile. Mimicking the approach of development teams offered a solution that made perfect sense. Post-It notes and whiteboards, whether physical or digital, are ubiquitous tools in agile and scrum project management. Their simplicity, flexibility, and effectiveness in fostering collaboration and visual management translate seamlessly to marketing teams.

Utilizing this visual method fosters a dynamic environment where change is not only anticipated but also welcomed, keeping operations fluid. A good manager always has their eye on the need for adjustments, where and when, in addition to shifting team priorities. Here's how it works.

Post-It notes are commonly placed on task boards (also known as Kanban boards) to visualize the workflow. These boards typically have columns representing different stages of the workflow, such as "Planned, To Do, In Progress, and Done." As work progresses, notes are moved across the columns.

In the world of sticky notes, change can be more seamless and immediate. During daily stand-up meetings, team members can use the notes to quickly and visually update others on the status of their tasks. Then as needed, with a simple rearrangement of the cards, a team can adjust priorities and course of action. New tasks can be added, priorities can be shifted, and everyone is on the same page quickly. This helps keep focus and alignment.

A simple kanban board

	Planned	To Do	In Progress	Done
Category 1	■	■ ■	■	
Category 2	□	■	■ ■	■
Category 3	■ ■			□ ■
Category 4	■ ■		■ □	■

By integrating these simple yet powerful tools, teams can improve their workflow management, enhance collaboration, and increase overall project transparency and effectiveness.

Don't be afraid to move on. Another big part of learning to pivot is not being afraid to move on – from ideas, projects, or outdated practices. The concept of moving on also applies to personal career growth. When the environment becomes stale, stifling or no longer aligns with your goals, having the confidence to move on can lead to new opportunities and growth.

Holding onto outdated strategies can hinder innovation. For example, a marketing campaign that once worked well might become ineffective over time. Continuously assessing and pivoting strategies helps maintain relevance in a dynamic market. Projects that no longer provide value should be reevaluated. This prevents resources from being wasted on initiatives that don't contribute to the company's goals. Understand that not all ideas or projects will succeed. Viewing failure as a learning opportunity can reduce the fear of moving on and encourage experimentation and innovation.

Try new things. Marketing thrives on creativity and innovation. It's about continuously finding fresh ways to engage with your audience and stand out in a crowded marketplace. As marketing professionals, staying on course with your strategic plan is essential, but it's equally important to inject innovation into your campaigns regularly. This dual approach ensures that your marketing efforts remain relevant and captivating.

Embracing experimentation can lead to discovering groundbreaking ideas that set your brand apart. Take the time to brainstorm and test new strategies, even if they deviate slightly from your usual tactics. This could involve leveraging emerging technologies, exploring new content formats, or tapping into underutilized channels. For example, consider how brands like Nike and Red Bull continuously push the envelope with creative campaigns that blend storytelling with innovative use of digital media. These brands understand that while a strong foundational strategy is critical, incorporating unique and unexpected elements keeps their marketing fresh and engaging.

> "You'll never be bored when you try something new. There's really no limit to what you can do." – Dr. Seuss

Encourage your team to think creatively and to not shy away from bold ideas. For example, did you know the first email marketing campaign was sent in 1978 by a marketing manager at Digital Equipment Corporation? A complete novelty at the time, the email sent to 400 people resulted in $13 million in sales. Remember though, not every new idea will work, but each experiment brings valuable insights that can refine and optimize your approach. As Steve Jobs famously said, "Innovation distinguishes between a leader and a follower." By balancing a solid strategic plan with a willingness to explore new opportunities, you ensure that your marketing efforts are both effective and dynamic, positioning your brand as a leader in the industry.

The Right Team, Tools, and Budget

The third floor is dedicated to being business savvy: understanding and leveraging the right mix of talent, resources, and financial support.

Marketing is undeniably a team sport, and one that needs equipment and money. Ensuring you have the best people, the appropriate tools, and adequate funding not only empowers your team but also drives the success of your initiatives. The more you grasp the dynamics of the right team, tools, and budget – the bigger advantage you'll have in succeeding.

The right team. Designing the perfect marketing organization involves creating a team that is balanced, collaborative, and capable of handling various aspects of marketing efficiently. Although the structure of marketing teams may vary greatly – from a single person to hundreds at large corporations - here's what I consider an ideal minimum structure for a mid-size B2B technology company. **If you're a Product Marketing Manager, you need this entire team working for you and your product.** The easier and more compelling you make it for them to incorporate your products and solutions, the easier it will be to achieve success.

- **Chief Marketing Officer:** Every marketing team needs an amazing leader. They oversee the entire marketing strategy, aligning it with business goals. They set the overall marketing direction, budget allocation, team leadership, cross-department collaboration, and ensure alignment with executive leadership.
- **Content Marketing Manager:** Content is still king. This key role is to manage the content strategy and execution. Responsibilities include editorial calendar, content creation and resource management, blog management, and collaboration with central subject matter experts.
- **Integrated Marketing Campaign Manager:** Orchestrating successful multi-dimensional marketing campaigns is an art and a science. This role focuses on creating and executing integrated marketing campaigns that build awareness, generate leads, and enable sales.
- **Product Marketing Manager**: Bridging the gap between product development, product management,

marketing and sales is essential. A product marketing manager does this well, in addition to go-to-market strategies, messaging, competitive analysis, product campaigns and launches, sales enablement, and more.
- **Marketing Operations Manager:** A systems and data magician, this role ensures the efficiency and effectiveness of marketing activities. Their role spans marketing automation, CRM management, data analysis, analyzing campaign performance reporting, optimizing marketing processes and ROI measurement.
- **Digital Marketing Manager:** Highly adaptable and detail-oriented, this tech-savvy role manages all digital marketing channels and strategies. Responsibilities cover SEO, SEM, PPC, social media marketing, digital advertisements, digital campaign execution, website management, and performance analysis and optimization.
- **Graphic and UI Designer:** This dedicated in-house resource can quickly collaborate with the team to create impressive visual content including marketing materials, website design, infographics, social media graphics, while helping to ensure a cohesive visual brand identity.
- **Field Marketing Manager:** With a passion for customer interaction and hands-on engagement in their region, this manager plans and executes events to build awareness, generate leads and enable sales. Their responsibilities cover trade shows, conferences, webinars, roadshows, and local marketing activities.
- **Influencer Relations Manager:** A professional communicator with socially aware interpersonal skills, they manage the company's public image and media relations including press releases, media outreach, handling PR crises, and maintaining relationships with journalists and influencers.

- **Customer Marketing Manager:** A passionate advocate for the customer experience, this position focuses on marketing to existing customers to drive retention and upsell. This can include areas such as customer success stories, loyalty programs, and engagement campaigns.

But what about agencies and external resources? Selecting the right agency is critically important but can be highly challenging - though that's a topic for another discussion. What's important here is to ensure you fully leverage agency resources available to you as a marketing lead.

- **Agency of record:** Ideally, your organization has invested in retaining a single creative agency that supports your brand by managing the company's brand identity, visual identity, brand guidelines, design, and digital presence.
- **Content creators:** Maintain a list of approved agencies or contractors who can be engaged on a project basis for specialized content creation, such as infographics, videos, and animations.
- **PR agency:** Partner with a PR agency that works with journalists, editors, influencers, and other media professionals to secure positive media coverage, including speaking engagements and award submissions. They ensure that not only do you get coverage, but that the coverage reflects the right messages.

The right tools. The collection of platforms and software applications used to create, execute, manage, and measure the results of marketing activities is known as the marketing technology, or martech, "stack." Martech stacks can range from quite simple to extremely complicated. To put things in perspective, chiefmartec.com shows that there are more than 14,106 martech applications available across 49 categories in the 2024 edition of their super graphic martech map[6]. That's quite a lot of options and choices.

Thus, it's important to remember that the more technology you add to your stack, the more expensive and complex your system becomes. So in the early stages, it may be best to consolidate it into the least number of tools possible. That's why tools like HubSpot are sometimes a good choice: it has everything you need in one platform to get the work done efficiently and productively. For most companies, a foundational technology infrastructure begins with:

- **Customer relationship management (CRM) software**: Tools like Salesforce or HubSpot for managing customer relationships and tracking sales leads.
- **Marketing automation**: Platforms like Marketo, Pardot, or HubSpot for automating marketing tasks and workflows, in addition to chatbot marketing platforms such as Drift.com, Botsify, or MobileMonkey.
- **Content management system (CMS)**: WordPress, Drupal, Contentful, HubSpot, or similar platforms for managing website content. For B2B companies, tools such as Highspot or Showpad are also highly desirable for sales content management.
- **Project management tool**: A tool such as Asana, Trello, Airtable, Smartsheet, or Monday.com for managing marketing projects and campaigns.
- **Social media platforms and tools**: Platforms such as LinkedIn, X (formerly Twitter), and YouTube, along with tools like Oktopost for scheduling social campaigns and encouraging employee advocacy.

---

[6] '2024 Marketing Technology Landscape', by Scott Brinker, chiefmartech.com, published May 7, 2024, https://chiefmartech.com/category/marketing-software.

Additional tools may include URL shorteners like bit.ly and social listening tools such as Mention.
- **Google Ads Management, Google Analytics, Google Search Console:** Essential tools for every digital marketing team.
- **Adtech tools:** Solutions like Demandbase for sending personalized online ads to target specific people at specific companies while fine-tuning the message.

Your organization's marketing and technical maturity will significantly influence the capabilities required for your company's martech stack. Additionally, beyond features and cost, several factors should be considered:

- **Team suitability**: Ensure the chosen products match your team's skills and available time. If a product is too complex, it will never be fully utilized and can become a huge source of frustration, resulting in a poor return on investment.
- **Integration**: Data movement is key. Verify that your products can easily integrate to allow critical data to flow seamlessly. If integration is difficult, you may need to develop customized integration code, which could be a costly endeavor.
- **Scalability**: Choose foundational elements that can support your company for 3-5 years. These elements must grow with the company to avoid the lengthy and complex process of swapping out systems, which can take as long as 6 to 18 months or more.

The right budget. Being budget savvy is not always the most exciting part of marketing. Quite truthfully, most of the time it is rather cumbersome and frustrating. But knowing the budgets and how your finance team operates puts you in a much better position to succeed.

The typical B2B marketing budget varies significantly based on factors such as company size, industry, and overall business objectives. **But many B2B companies allocate between 5-10% of their total revenue to marketing.** This percentage can vary based on the company's growth stage and competitive environment, in addition to what they include or exclude.

Here's a sample breakdown of what a typical B2B marketing budget might look like:

- **Digital marketing (40-50%)**: This primarily includes your digital ad spend, such as Google Ads, Google Display Network, and ads on social platforms like LinkedIn and X (formerly Twitter). It also covers account-based marketing (ABM) advertisements and content syndication.
- **Field marketing events and webinars (20-30%)**: This encompasses trade shows, conferences, customer seminars, webinars, and virtual events. It also includes any related regional-specific customizations or needs.
- **Content creation and management (10-20%)**: This covers all areas of content creation and management, including third-party resources and external agencies used to develop content assets.
- **Technology and tools (5-10%)**: This budget area is for your martech stack—the platforms and software applications previously discussed. It typically also covers any development support for the website.
- **Public relations and communications (5-10%)**: This section includes analyst relations (subscription fees), influencer relations expenses, awards and speaker fees, media distribution expenses (such as Business Wire), agency retainers, and more.
- **Miscellaneous – i.e., brand, customer marketing (5-10%)**: This section includes brand, design, and creative services (retainer for the agency of record), subscriptions to creative services (photos and videos,

etc.), and swag. Customer marketing covers expenses related to retention and loyalty programs.

However, it's rarely that simple. For instance, some sources quote marketing expenses as high as 11% of revenue, while others suggest a more modest range of 2-5%. Then there's the question of exactly what that percentage includes, meaning does it include headcount? Headcount, or cost of labor, encompasses total compensation for the marketing team, plus any travel expenses. Total compensation not only includes salary, but also includes benefits and overhead, often estimated to be 1.25 to 1.4 times a base salary. This covers health insurance, retirement contributions, taxes, and other employee benefits.

Additionally, the allocation of budget categories tends to skew once applied in practice. Here's a couple of examples. First up, the event budget. It typically runs much higher than desired, especially as a single large event can consume a significant portion of the budget.

Second up, the content creation budget. It may be well-funded, but content creation is extremely time-consuming, even with the use of external resources. As a result, the team may struggle to execute all the desired assets, leaving the budget underutilized.

Third up, the public relations budget might seem straightforward, but in the B2B world, analyst memberships with firms like Gartner and Forrester can be quite costly. This budget often carries a much larger price tag than anticipated.

Fourth up, in the miscellaneous category which includes brand and customer marketing, the retainer for an agency of record typically resides here (that can be $10k to 20k per month), leaving little room for customer communications and advocacy programs.

Lastly, in today's digital landscape, the martech stack has become indispensable. As a company grows, this area requires significant investment. Ensuring the right technology is in place is crucial for supporting marketing efforts and driving growth.

So, if you apply this sample budget breakdown to a B2B company with $250 million in revenue, and veer to account for these types of scenarios, it may look something more like this:

- **Total marketing budget: $5,000,000 (2% of revenue)**
- **Less headcount expense: 1,750,000 (35% of total budget)**

- **Equals the effective marketing budget: $3,250,000**
- Digital marketing: $975,000 (30%)
- Field marketing events and webinars: $812,500 (25%)
- Content creation and management: $325,000 (10%)
- Technology and tools: $487,500 (15%)
- Public relations and communications: $422,500 (13%)
- Miscellaneous: $227,500 (7%)

On last thought. Sometimes there are also areas that typically may be covered in a product management budget, such as industry and technical memberships, competitive research, or expenses related to product design and usability – that can creep over to the marketing budget too.

Bottom line, by carefully structuring the marketing budget and ensuring that your plan's critical categories are adequately funded, you can more effectively drive growth, optimize resources, and achieve your strategic objectives. This approach allows for balanced investment across key areas, **ensuring that no critical component is missing nor underfunded** and that your marketing efforts yield the best possible return on investment. Three things to stay grounded in:

- The marketing budget should **align closely with the overall business strategy and goals**, ensuring that all marketing efforts contribute to the company's growth and success.
- The budget should always be **flexible**, to adapt to shifts in company performance, changing market conditions, and emerging opportunities.
- It's then essential to continuously measure the **return on investment** for different marketing activities to optimize budget allocation.

Beware of energy vampires.

In the realms of team, tools, and budget, there are often forces at play that are exhausting, drain energy, distract focus, and hinder productivity. These are the energy vampires.

Certain individuals might immediately come to mind:

- **The know-it-all**: This person acts as if they have superior knowledge and dismisses others' ideas, contributions, and situations. They seem to like to hear themselves speak and only want to do things their way.
- **The complainer**: Constantly focusing on the negative, this individual drags down team morale. They respond to new initiatives or change with skepticism and criticism, rarely offering constructive feedback.
- **The blame shifter**: This individual avoids responsibility by blaming others for mistakes and failures. A lead who accuses team members of not working hard enough when a deadline is missed, despite their own poor planning, illustrates this behavior.

- **The drama queen/king**: Thriving on conflict and drama, often over trivial matters, this person disrupts the workplace. A co-worker who blows minor issues out of proportion, causing unnecessary stress and tension, is typical of this type.
- **The brown-noser**: Excessively flattering and agreeing with superiors to gain favor, often at the expense of peers. An employee who agrees with every suggestion the boss makes, regardless of its merit, and frequently undermines colleagues to appear more loyal.
- **The passive-aggressive**: Indirectly expressing negative feelings, this person creates confusion and tension. It may appear as sarcasm, or back-handed compliments, and can feel intimidating and manipulating.

These types of toxic co-workers cost you time, energy, and at times, your sanity. But by recognizing and identifying them, you can then develop strategies to mitigate their negative impact on the workplace. A healthy and productive work environment is a must. If these types of energy vampires become rampant in your space, it may be time to move on.

There are energy vampires in systems too—platforms that are not a good fit. Either they have the wrong functionality, are too time consuming to learn, are repetitive to other systems already in place, or simply do not add value for the time required to engage with them. In this case, it's important to voice your opinion confidently, but recognize that some battles aren't worth your time. Utilize these systems minimally and focus elsewhere.

The key lesson is to honestly evaluate your team, systems, and tools, and only focus on areas where you can thrive and drive results. For example, as a product marketing manager, concentrate your budget on product launches, integrated campaigns, and sales enablement content, leaving data sheets, training, and competitive research to others on the product side. Then recognize potential agitations that detract from what's important. Identify those energy vampires and carry metaphorical garlic to keep them at bay.

UX is Really Just Good Marketing

As we reach the fourth floor, the focus shifts to customer experience. This level is about striving to exceed customer expectations, making every interaction count.

User experience (UX) embraces the art and science of user interaction. But it's not just about making interfaces easy and engaging to use. It's about knowing who your market is, what is important to them, why it is important to them - **and then designing accordingly**. It encompasses all aspects of the end-user's interaction with the company, its services, and its products. Driving not only acquisition, but also adoption, retention, and advocacy. It is why companies such as Google, Apple, Amazon, Disney, and other industry leaders continue to outperform.

UX design opportunities span the entire customer journey. Although not all companies do, good marketers care about UX across all touchpoints.

Beginning with customer acquisition, and perhaps the most obvious, your UX design efforts include website design, landing pages, SEO and accessibility, advertisements, social media and more. For example:

- **Landing pages**: Create engaging, informative, and visually appealing landing pages that capture attention and drive conversions. Use clear call-to-actions (CTAs) and minimalistic design to keep the focus on conversion goals.

- **SEO and accessibility:** Ensure the website is optimized for search engines and accessible to users with disabilities, enhancing discoverability and user experience.
- **Social media ads:** Utilize platform-specific design guidelines to create ads that stand out on social media feeds, encouraging clicks and engagement.

The acquisition experience should then seamlessly connect into the customer adoption stage. Many times, I've seen a disconnect here between product and marketing teams regarding continuity and collaboration. When marketing is connected to product design, customer retention and advocacy – the result is uniquely noticeable in a positive way.

- **Product digital design:** Developing intuitive onboarding processes is essential for guiding new users through the initial setup and highlighting key features of the product. This involves creating a user-friendly interface with logical navigation, ensuring users can easily understand and utilize the product effectively.
- **Industrial design:** For physical products, it's important to ensure they are ergonomically designed, aesthetically pleasing, and easy to use. Additionally, the packaging design should not only be attractive but also functional and environmentally friendly, enhancing the overall product experience.
- **Customer communication marketing streams:** Email marketing should involve designing engaging and personalized email templates to keep customers informed and interested in product updates, promotions, and content. Push notifications should be non-intrusive, timely, and relevant, providing value without being disruptive.
- **Customer service:** A comprehensive, easy-to-navigate help center with FAQs, tutorials, and

troubleshooting guides is crucial. Additionally, designing intelligent chatbots and user-friendly live chat interfaces can provide immediate assistance and enhance customer support.
- **Reward programs:** Loyalty programs should be easy to understand and participate in, with clear rewards and benefits that encourage repeat business. Implementing gamification elements such as points, badges, and leaderboards can make the loyalty program more engaging and fun.
- **Customer advocacy:** Creating seamless and attractive referral programs incentivizes customers to refer friends and family. Encouraging user-generated content (UGC) allows customers to create and share content related to your product. Designing platforms or features that make it easy for them to contribute (and for you to showcase their content) can greatly enhance customer advocacy.

This structured approach ensures that each aspect is thoughtfully considered and effectively implemented. By addressing UX design at every stage of the customer journey, businesses can create a cohesive and satisfying experience that not only attracts and converts new customers but also retains and nurtures them into loyal advocates.

Find Your Sweet Spot

Finally, the top floor represents self-awareness: discovering what you like best - and are best at.

A very savvy and grounded colleague of mine once referred to it as finding your sweet spot. It's a process that involves pausing to reflect on your unique strengths and weaknesses, likes and dislikes, to truly discover what you excel at and enjoy the most in your chosen profession. Identifying your own sweet spot can lead to greater job satisfaction, enhanced productivity, and a more meaningful career.

No one is better than you, at being you.

Consider the marketer who thrives on creativity and innovation. Their sweet spot might be in developing groundbreaking campaigns that challenge the status quo, rather than sticking to traditional, tried-and-true methods. They might find the most fulfillment working in industries that value and reward inventive thinking, such as technology or fashion. Their passion for new ideas and problem-solving enables them to excel in roles that require constant adaptation and creative strategies.

Another example is someone who excels in analytical thinking and enjoys working with data. This person might find their sweet spot in roles that involve market research, data analysis, and optimization of marketing campaigns based on insights. They might prefer working in sectors like finance or healthcare, where data-driven decision-making is crucial. By leveraging their analytical skills, they can provide valuable insights that drive business growth and improve marketing effectiveness.

It's also essential to consider the work environment and team dynamics. Some professionals thrive in small, close-knit teams where they can take on multiple roles and have a significant impact. Others might prefer larger organizations where they can specialize and collaborate with diverse teams across various departments. Understanding these preferences helps in finding roles that align with personal working styles and maximize contributions to the team's success.

Moreover, identifying your sweet spot can also mean understanding your preferred style of tackling challenges. For instance, if you are someone who thrives on taking on tough challenges and solving complex problems, you might find your niche in turnaround projects or startups where your skills are crucial for overcoming obstacles and driving growth.

Reflecting on these aspects helps in carving out a career path that not only plays to your strengths but also brings joy and fulfillment. As Steve Jobs famously said, "The only way to do great work is to love what you do." By discovering and operating within your sweet spot, you can achieve remarkable success and make a meaningful impact in your field. Whether it's through creative innovation, analytical prowess, or problem-solving skills, finding your sweet spot allows you to leverage your unique talents and passions, leading to a more rewarding and impactful career.

I've also discovered that this self-awareness naturally provides a roadmap to you for continual learning. By understanding your strengths, weaknesses, likes, and dislikes, you can make informed decisions about where to focus your learning efforts. Investing in yourself in this way not only furthers your professional growth but also ensures a more satisfying and dynamic career trajectory.

Invest in Yourself – the Power of Lifelong Learning

Continual learning is not just a professional necessity; it's a personal growth strategy that can have profound impacts on both your career and your life. The list of reasons why is compelling and convincing.

- **Fuel for adaptability**: The world is evolving rapidly, and learning ensures you can adapt to modern technologies, methodologies, and industry trends. Embracing change becomes more manageable when you view learning as a constant.
- **Professional relevance**: In a dynamic job market, staying relevant is crucial. Continuous learning

ensures that your skills and knowledge remain up to date, making you an asset to employers and industries.
- **Personal growth and sense of accomplishment**: Learning extends beyond the workplace. Whether it's a new language, a musical instrument, or a hobby, acquiring new skills enriches your life, provides a sense of accomplishment, and keeps your mind active.
- **Enhanced problem-solving**: Cultivate critical thinking. Learning exposes you to diverse perspectives and fosters critical thinking. The ability to approach problems with a well-rounded and informed mindset is invaluable both professionally and personally.
- **Increased confidence**: Embrace challenges. The more you learn, the more confident you become. This confidence extends to tackling new challenges, taking on leadership roles, and pursuing opportunities you might have otherwise hesitated to explore.
- **Networking opportunities**: Learning often involves interacting with a community of learners. This community can provide valuable networking opportunities, fostering relationships that can lead to mentorship, collaborations, and career advancements.
- **Career flexibility**: Learning opens doors to new career paths. It allows you to pivot, when necessary, explore different industries, or even start your own venture. The broader your skill set, the more flexible and resilient your career becomes.
- **Curiosity:** Cultivating a curious mindset keeps life interesting. The joy of discovery and the pursuit of knowledge bring fulfillment and prevent professional stagnation.
- **Personal branding**: Continuous learning is a testament to your commitment to growth. It enhances your personal brand, positioning you as

someone who is forward-thinking, adaptable, and invested in personal and professional development.
- **Investing in yourself**: Lifelong learning is an investment in yourself. Recognize that the journey of learning is ongoing, and each new piece of knowledge contributes to your personal and professional development.
- **Navigating uncertainty**: Learning builds resilience. In times of uncertainty or career challenges, individuals with a strong learning mindset are better equipped to navigate ambiguity and come out stronger on the other side.

And today, the opportunities for continuing your education are more abundant and accessible than ever before. Unlike in the past, where options were limited to traditional classroom settings, we now have a wealth of online courses, mini-MBA programs, and certification programs at our fingertips. These modern platforms offer flexibility, a wide range of subjects, and the ability to learn from industry experts without geographical constraints. Whether you're looking to upskill in your current marketing field or explore new areas, the resources available today are so much easier and more convenient.

So go ahead and approach learning with enthusiasm, embrace it as a lifelong endeavor, and I think you'll find that it not only propels your career forward - but adds immeasurable value to your personal growth and fulfillment.

As a final note, there's three things I would encourage you to remember.

First, in today's fast-paced and ever-evolving business landscape, marketing has become way too complex to navigate without a well-defined plan. Having a solid blueprint to help organize and curate your marketing initiatives can serve as a strategic guide to mastering the complexities and seizing the opportunities.

Secondly, remember to always "look up"—elevate your perspective to see beyond the immediate tasks and align your efforts with the broader vision.

And lastly, and perhaps most importantly, be sure to embrace your passion for marketing. Let the thrill of creativity, the challenge of problem-solving, and the joy of connecting with your audience keep you positively energized.

###

Good luck to you
as you paint your own adventure
in the colorful and vibrant world of marketing.
Thanks for your time.
I wish you much success!

About the Author

 **Amy Mikolasy** has over 25 years of marketing, product development, and leadership experience within the telecommunications, wireless, and technology industry in both start-ups and large corporate environments.

Throughout her career, she's continued a creative passion for visual design and evangelizing new technology and innovation, including rich technical solutions in global markets.

Amy holds a Bachelor of Science degree in business administration and marketing from the University of Illinois at Champaign-Urbana, in addition to completion of continuing education programs at Southern Methodist University Dallas, School of Engineering for project management and at Rutgers University Business School NJ, Mini-MBA program for digital marketing. She is currently enjoying an endless summer in south Florida.

Think Indigo

Index

agility, 36, 121-124
artificial intelligence, 54
Beadman, Jessica, 97
brand, 11-12
budget, 129-133
business savvy, 124
buyer persona, 23-25
campaigns
    framework, 43-46
    global, 38, 45
    product, 45, 102
    tactics and integration, 55
content
    audit, 47-48
    storytelling, 48-50
    types of, 50-53
competitive differentiation, 27-31
customer buying cycle, 46
demand generation, 12-13
design, 84
details, in execution, 90
digital marketing, 56
Einbinder, Saul, 6
energy vampires, 133
elevator pitch, 32
field marketing, 69, 111
go-to-market (GTM), 93-102
influencer relations, 67
kanban board, 122
keywords, 34-35
landing pages, 64
learning, continuous, 137

looking up, 116
martech stack, tools, 127
marchitecture, 43
messaging framework, 31-35
metrics, 72-79
personal branding, 118-120, 140
pragmatic marketing framework, 94
product launches, 93-102
    campaigns, 102
    readiness kit, 98-102
    timeline, 100
product naming, 103-107
public relations, 67
re-targeting, 63
return-on-investment (ROI), 1, 17-19, 76
sales enablement, 14-17, 107-113
Scheafer, Mark W., 120
Schorsch, Peter, 43
search engine optimization (SEO), 34, 53, 62
self-awareness, 137
social media, 62
strategic priorities, 38
target audience, 20-26
team, 124
use cases, 25-26
user experience, 135-137
value proposition, 27-31
Viscomi, Mary Jane, 91

Printed in Great Britain
by Amazon

4194afcf-992b-4773-b2fd-cd4275a60c91R01